PROUSTIAN UNCERTAINTIES

PROUSTIAN UNCERTAINTIES

ON

READING

AND

REREADING

IN SEARCH OF LOST TIME

Saul Friedländer

OTHER PRESS
New York

Production editor: Yvonne E. Cárdenas
Text designer: Jennifer Daddio/Bookmark Design & Media Inc.
This book was set in Dante MT and Trade Gothic by
Alpha Design & Composition of Pittsfield, NH

1 3 5 7 9 10 8 6 4 2

Library of Congress Cataloging-in-Publication Data
Names: Friedländer, Saul, 1932- author.
Title: Proustian uncertainties : on reading and rereading In search of lost time / Saul Friedländer.
Description: New York : Other Press, [2020] | Includes bibliographical references.
Identifiers: LCCN 2020012475 (print) | LCCN 2020012476 (ebook) | ISBN 9781590519110 (hardcover) | ISBN 9781590519127 (ebook)
Subjects: LCSH: Proust, Marcel, 1871-1922. À la recherche du temps perdu. | Proust, Marcel, 1871-1922—Criticism and interpretation. | Memory in literature. | Identity (Philosophical concept) in literature.
Classification: LCC PQ2631.R63 .A7914 2020 (print) | LCC PQ2631.R63 (ebook) | DDC 843/.912—dc23
LC record available at https://lccn.loc.gov/2020012475
LC ebook record available at https://lccn.loc.gov/2020012476

This book is dedicated to

ZEEV STERNHELL

who passed away in Jerusalem in June 2020.

Zeev was a powerful voice for peace and justice.

He was an expert on fascism, especially fascism in France.

And for me he was a wonderful friend.

CONTENTS

PROUSTIAN UNCERTAINTIES

INTRODUCTION

P roust?" a French acquaintance asked me when told
about my endeavor. "Why Proust?" My answer had
been vague, and the question was to the point: why
Proust? The vagueness of the answer was also to the point:
I couldn't tell clearly why I had decided to work on Proust,
or maybe I didn't want to tell. One thing was sure: I had not
the competence and certainly not the intention of becoming one more "specialist" of Proust. And yet my desire to
write specifically on *À la recherche* was not haphazard; I was
certain about that. Was it due to the beauty of *In Search*?
Its complexity? Without any doubt those aspects played a
role, mainly in my rereading *In Search* time and time again.
But wasn't there more? Wasn't I rereading it because it re-
sponded to some need, to something in my personal life
that called for delving into that book, something that was

intimately attuned to it? Some themes in the novel were close to my own ruminations over the decades, mainly about identity.

Whatever the motivation may have been, I started re-reading *In Search* with particular attention. Soon I noticed aspects that I had failed to see before, and as I soon realized after some inquiry, seemed to have generally escaped attention. Of course, I felt once more the extraordinary pull of a text that, as for so many other readers, was not only the greatest novel of French literature but one of the most important novels ever written.

Given that there is hardly any plot, *In Search* is easily summed up: it is the life story of a Narrator whose main desire since childhood has been to become a writer. As he doubts his literary talent, he spends decades of his adulthood in idleness, devoting himself to social climbing from his middle-class background into the highest reaches of the French aristocracy. It is only in late adulthood that he discovers, by pure chance, through a kind of epiphany triggered by a surge of involuntary memory, that he has the creative literary gift that will allow him to fulfill his ambition. He then starts writing the story of his life that will, in great part, tell what he remembers from his years of idleness, years that, unknown to him, have been in fact years of preparation. From then on, his writing will indeed be a search for lost time, which in the original French is both "time forgotten that has to be discovered again" and "time squandered that has to be retrieved or regained."

While the Narrator tells us that as far as writing went, he remained inactive until late in adult life, possibly to add importance to the quasi-magic impact of involuntary memory, Proust himself, although fixated on social climbing and plagued by sporadic illness, wrote assiduously during all these years: short stories, published when he was twenty-five, in 1896, under the title *Les plaisirs et les jours* (*Pleasures and Days*); a novel some eight hundred pages long (*Jean Santeuil*), unpublished during his lifetime; another book of literary criticism that also contained fragments of a novel (*Contre Sainte-Beuve*), also published only posthumously; and various lighter articles for newspapers and journals, mainly pastiches of well-known authors. Remarkably, all these early writings, the published and the unpublished, include an ever-growing number of themes that will reappear in the great novel, which he started sometime in 1909 (the last two volumes were only published after the author's death in 1922, at age fifty-one).

The time "squandered" by the Narrator gave us, the readers, the extraordinary descriptions of French society during the Belle Epoque, particularly of the high bourgeoisie (the Verdurins and their salon) and the aristocracy at its highest reaches, the Faubourg Saint-Germain (represented by several salons, but mainly by that of the Duc and the Duchesse de Guermantes). The Narrator doesn't subject us to social analysis but in a constant flow of observations, moving from the magnificent homes and material surroundings of the quasi-mythic aristocratic families to their personalities, presents their taste, their silliness, and their nastiness, particularly as expressed by their conversations.

According to Walter Benjamin, the German-Jewish emigrant living in Paris, the French novelist and political figure Maurice Barrès described *In Search* as the work of "A Persian poet in a porter's lodge" (Benjamin, "The Image of Proust," *Illuminations*, 209). This amusing description isn't off the mark. One of the most striking aspects of the novel resides indeed in the endless conversations that unveil with extraordinary subtlety (the Persian poet's subtlety and not the porter's one) the psychological characteristics of the main characters that populate the Narrator's world. Incidentally, not all great minds enjoyed that subtlety. According to his recent biographer, de Gaulle told his son that he did not like Proust's preciousness, his contorted style, and his artificial milieu, where the main point of existence was society dinners (Jackson, *De Gaulle*, 712).

The story unfolds on many levels, particularly at that of social description, as just mentioned, but also, constantly, at that of the Narrator's personal reactions, observations, choices, and feelings. At this personal level there is much passion and pain, and weaved throughout the emotional twists and turns, magnificent evocations of nature, the arts, literature, and, among so many other different microcosms, the street sounds of Paris waking up to a new day.

We receive the narration from a fictional avatar who recalls the course of his own life from childhood to the moment, decades later, when he feels able to start writing. The

Narrator's memories follow very closely the author's biography. My attention will be directed to those issues in the avatar's text that, as mentioned, seem not to have been noticed but which appear crucial to me. But my interpretations will not always remain within the confines of the text; at times they will lead from the text to the author's personal world, and often from that world to a further understanding of the text.

This back-and-forth from text to author and from author to text characterizes the core of my approach and demands some further explanation. On a number of crucial issues, the fictional Narrator swerves away from his biographical model and offers weird statements, contradicting what we know of the author's life: such discrepancies are manifestly intentional. Then, however, at times very soon after and in other cases hundreds of pages later, a small detail is mentioned that affirms the opposite of previous statements. For some reason, the Narrator's strange, contradictory statements haven't drawn enough attention among Proust's scholars.

My aim, of course, will not be to figure out solely what the Narrator means, but to investigate what he seems to mean, or hide, in order to understand the author's sly hints or attempts at camouflage by using the Narrator's statements. And, it will be from that angle, by trying to decipher the author's strategy on the basis of the Narrator's equivocations, that I will approach the major themes, as well as some other issues, less important in the context of this essay.

One may counter that *In Search* is a work of fiction, that the Narrator is a wholly invented character whose autobiography, points of view, and attitudes—whether closely mirroring those of the author or in complete opposition to them—should be considered entirely independent of him. Proust himself asserted on several occasions that the life story told by the Narrator had nothing to do with his own life, and quite a few commentators followed him in this. Yet in other instances he admitted that the story told by the Narrator was in many respects very close to his own life. It is this second interpretation that I have adopted: the Narrator's story is not Proust's autobiography, but it is close enough, as I hope to show, to allow for the questions I will be asking. A number of interpreters also adopt this position.

In George D. Painter's biography of the 1960s, for example, there is hardly any character or event described in the novel (even minor characters, secondary events, and earlier writings) that cannot claim an original in the author's life. That said, the Narrator creates composite portraits or somewhat twists the rendition of events, but we cannot dismiss Painter's erudite references, even if it became clear over time that corrections were necessary.

William C. Carter's more recent biography offers a very nuanced assessment of the proximity between author and Narrator: "In his letters and notes to himself about the novel, Proust usually spoke of the Narrator as 'I,' making no distinction between himself and his fictional persona...Still, Proust was engaged not in writing his autobiography but in creating a novel in which there are strong autobiographical elements. The symbiosis between Proust and his Narrator can be explained by the hybrid origin of the story. Having begun as an essay in which the 'I' was himself, as the text veered more and more toward fiction, the 'I' telling the story became both its generator and its subject, like a Siamese twin, intimately linked to Proust's body and soul and yet other" (Carter, *Marcel Proust: A Life*, 474). Further on in the biography, Carter adds an important comment: "As Proust lived more and more in the world he invented, he came to embody the Narrator rather than the other way around" (ibid., 603). Another biographer, Jean-Yves Tadié, put it succinctly: "It is extraordinary to see how Proust allows nothing of his life to be wasted. One might well suppose, then, that one could put a real name to each character, a real event to each event in his fiction" (Tadié, foreword to Marcel Proust, *Letters to His Neighbor*, 12).

As for Proust himself, on occasion he forgot his own admonitions and recognized a close similarity between *In Search* and his life. In a letter of November 1913 to René Blum, a friend of his first publisher, Bernard Grasset, he evoked, for example, the discovery brought about by the taste of a piece of cake dipped in a cup of tea: "thus part of the book is a part of my life that I had forgotten and that I suddenly discover again in eating a piece of madeleine dipped in tea, a taste that ravishes me before I had recognized and identified it, as I used to eat some of it every morning in the far away past [*jadis*]; thereupon my life of that time resurrects...All people and gardens of those years of my life are born from a cup of tea" (Proust, *Lettres*, 637, my translation).

The overarching issue of this essay will be the question of identity, particularly that of the part-Jewish identity of the Narrator and, less thoroughly so, that of his homosexuality. How does the Narrator define himself? We know, for example, that the author did not hide his homosexuality, but the Narrator did. Why the difference? We know that the Narrator tried to marginalize his part-Jewish background. Does it reflect the author's position, and how does the Narrator handle what he tries but does not manage to dismiss?

These are major questions raised by the text and reflected in the text to which the author's life doesn't give obvious answers. And this isn't all. The Narrator's reflections on time, on death, on memory, and on love, as well as the many paths leading to the image of self that he projects— do they mirror what we know about the author's perceptions? The menu offers quite a few dishes, but the meal hasn't yet been cooked . . . And as the Narrator is the chef, I decided to designate him with a capital.

I am writing in English (as I did for several previous books), which in this case may look somewhat eccentric; it requires using a translation of Proust's novel and other texts. It seems that at this point (2017 and beyond) the most frequently and preferably utilized translation of *In Search of Lost Time*—and the one I will use—is the one published by Modern Library in North America. This is C. K. Scott Moncrieff's, successively amended by Terence Kilmartin, D. J. Enright, and Andreas Mayor to incorporate corrections and additions introduced by the French editors into the original text. One of the most remarkable aspects of this translation, it seems to me, is the rendition of Proust's sumptuous style and its unusually long but characteristic sentences into a language that typically favors short, declarative sentences, without losing the poetry of it all.

.1.

FAMILY MATTERS

Marcel Proust's mother, Jeanne Weill, was the love of his life. In the novel, she is also the Narrator's major love; there, however, she is represented by two figures: the grandmother, who is the source and the object of undiluted love, and the mother, who increasingly becomes a target of resentment over time.

From the outset of *In Search*, the Narrator recaptures the intense relation between mother and child. Yet, nowhere in the novel do we learn his parents' names, nor do we get even a hint of their physical appearance, with the exception of the grandmother's gray hair.

Quite often in the novel there is no detailed physical description of even significant characters—with some exceptions, of course. However, a few details are always offered. The evocation of their likeness on the stained-glass windows of a church or among some Renaissance portraits gives, in the Narrator's view, an indirect but sufficient notion of their appearance. More generally, the Narrator, a staunch enemy of realism, probably believed that the mention of some physical traits was enough, maybe the eye color, the curve of a nose, a hairdo, a gaze, mainly some favored posture, at times jewels, clothes, and, above all, behavior and conversation. The conversations are so vivid, the characters' behavior is so perfectly sketched, that even without any elaborate physical description you see all of them as if you had lived among them for a long time. Paradoxically, some characters of no significance, those who have nothing to say, those who are mere extras, probably the majority of the hundreds of people appearing in the novel, sometimes receive a more detailed physical description than the more important ones.

One gets the impression that the author, possibly the greatest painter in words in French literature, takes pleasure at times in evoking such bit players, either directly or by using the most unexpected and most striking metaphors, and often by using both, in the same minimalist yet unforgettable rendition. Here, for example, is somebody of no importance, the Marquis de Palancy, whom the Narrator notices in the Princesse de Guermantes's box at the theater, just before the great Berma is about to come onstage:

"The Marquis de Palancy, his face bent downwards at the end of his long neck, his round bulging eye glued to the glass of his monocle, moved slowly around in the transparent shade and appeared no more to see the public in the stalls than a fish that drifts past, unconscious of the press of curious gazers, behind the glass wall of an aquarium. Now and again he paused, venerable, wheezing, moss-grown, and the audience could not have told whether he was in pain, asleep, swimming, about to spawn, or merely taking breath" (*Search*, III, 48).

Yet, regarding the Narrator's parents, nothing of the kind exists; and this peculiar reticence doesn't stop there. While the Narrator offers lengthy direct quotes of most of the characters' conversations, either with him or among themselves, we hear much less of what is directly expressed by the parents to each other, except when the father ventures comments about a dinner guest, the former diplomat, the Marquis de Norpois. The relations between the parents are affectionate, possibly in a somewhat one-sided way: the mother, the Narrator tells, "knew that she was carrying out that wifely duty which consisted in making life pleasant and comfortable for her husband, just as when she saw to it that his dinner was perfectly cooked and served in silence" (*Search*, II, 10). There was also admiration on her part, which she never failed to express, about her husband's talents, even minor ones, such as the ability to find his way in the modest outlay of paths near Combray, the village where the family oftentimes spent its summer vacations. As we shall see, the Narrator's feelings for his father were somewhat different from those of the mother. Be it as it may, the parents disappear from *In Search*, the father first, then the mother, without leaving a trace. How long did they remain alive? We do not know.

The role of the Narrator's father in the novel is minor. Apart from being a disciplinarian, the father often showed "coldness and reserve" (*Search*, I, 106) and was prone to sudden outbursts that terrified the family: "[He] would never inform us of any decision except in a manner calculated to cause us a maximum of agitation, out of all proportion to the decision itself. So that it was easy for him to call us absurd for appearing so distressed by so small a matter, our distress corresponding in reality to the perturbation that he had aroused in us. And if...these arbitrary whims of my father's had been passed on to me to complement the sensitive nature to which they had so long remained alien and, throughout my whole childhood, had caused so much suffering, that sensitive nature informed them very exactly as to the points at which they could most effectively be aimed" (*Search*, V, 138). All this doesn't mean that the Narrator didn't occasionally also have kind words for his father when he showed some understanding for the desires and aspirations of his son: "My father's words caused me great uneasiness. His unexpected kindnesses, when they occurred, had always made me long to kiss his glowing cheeks above his beard, and if I did not yield to the impulse, it was simply because I was afraid of annoying him" (*Search*, II, 73). The most famous such occasion, which I will describe further on, is that of the mother's special evening kiss, benevolently allowed by the father, contrary to his usual behavior.

Although both parents disappear from the novel without a trace, the mother's pedigree is amply displayed due to the major role played by her own mother, the Narrator's maternal grandmother; even the slightly anti-Semitic maternal grandfather has his place among the Combray characters. About the father's parents, the Narrator hasn't even a word to spare; they do not exist.

Moreover, in the Narrator's eyes, the father appears as somewhat ridiculous from the outset, with the meteorological preoccupations and the pathfinding talents he displayed in Combray and, later on, with his obsessive ambition to be elected to the "Institut." What was his profession? We don't know with any precision. We only vaguely grasp that he was a high civil servant, somehow linked to foreign affairs, because he was in close, semi-official contact with the retired ambassador the Marquis de Norpois, and sat with him in various commissions (In a chance remark by a friend of the Narrator's grandmother, we are told that the Narrator's father is the Permanent Secretary of the Ministry, which would turn him into a very high official indeed) (Search, II, 381).

The Narrator makes sure that the reader recognizes the real father, a well-known physician, under the mask of an eminent colleague, Dr. Cottard, who becomes professor and member of the Academy of Medicine like Papa Proust, and, apart from his medical ability, is described as something of an imbecile. The Narrator sums up his opinion of the father in declaring, as an aside, that he "was a simple soul" (*Search*, II, 710).

In the almost one thousand pages of the manuscript fragments of a novel, discovered and published only in the early 1950s, written by Marcel between his twenty-fourth and twenty-eighth year and entitled *Jean Santeuil* by the publisher, we discover an early version of the autobiographical quasi-fiction that some ten years later will turn into *In Search*. In that early work the author expresses at great length his love for his mother, not without some passing disagreements, and his very mixed feelings about his father, whose explosions of anger he describes and whose foibles he openly makes fun of. Thus, Papa Proust's hunger for titles and recognition becomes in the novel an accumulation of ridiculous official functions, such as "vice president of the [government] commission for quinoa grains and secretary of the commission for suburban wretchedness" (*Jean Santeuil*, 80–81). This early, tentative novel confirms the author's feelings, notwithstanding expressions of affection once the parents had grown old.

The nonexistence of Proust's brother Robert in *Search* may be interpreted as a compounding element of the Narrator's attitude toward the father, as Robert followed in his footsteps and became a respected surgeon who showed great courage during the First World War, in a field hospital close to the front. Moreover, Robert took as much care as possible of the author's deteriorating health: he was a surrogate father in many ways, and ignored by the Narrator.

One last detail: Proust's father, Adrien, died in November 1903, of the sequel of a cerebral hemorrhage that struck him down in the toilets of the Faculty of Medicine, where he had gone to preside over an examination jury (Tadié, *Proust*, 425). As we shall see further on, the Narrator describes the onset of his grandmother's fatal illness as having occurred in public toilets on the Champs-Elysées. For Proust's biographer Jean-Yves Tadié, there was no intention of "defiling" the mother by using that scene, as nothing of the kind did happen to her, nor to her mother. Rather, in Tadié's words, Proust tried "to control through his writing the painful memory that pursued him of his father being struck down in a lavatory" (Tadié, *Proust*, 425). Tadié's suggestion is merely an assumption regarding the author's reticence. Given the Narrator's general attitude toward the father, it could be anything else but his attempt to overcome a painful memory through writing. Who was being defiled if not the father? In any case, demeaning the father and eliminating the brother leaves Marcel as the only worthy recipient of Mamma's love.

According to some biographers, the mother's disappearance and the absence of any description of her death in the novel (Jeanne Weill died from uremia in 1905) was also due to the inability of the author to face it. In fact, from the Narrator's perspective, as the intense love between mother and son is partly shared between grandson and maternal grandmother, it could be that the son's supposed inability to describe the mother's death led to the description of the grandmother's terminal illness in *The Guermantes Way*. The identity of the fatal illness, uremia, is an indication of the Narrator's intent. Some of this description is padded by detailed, mostly sarcastic, portraits of the physicians who successively appear at the grandmother's bedside and—what is more unexpected—by lengthy digressions about the servant Françoise's psychology and behavior. Incidentally, the description of the physicians is another jab directed at the father: either they are competent but otherwise ridiculously pompous (Dieulafoy); good diagnosticians but downright stupid, as with Cottard; or intelligent and well-read but totally wrong in their diagnosis (du Boulbon).

The most intense expression of the bond between mother and son is presented close to the beginning of the novel. Even if they haven't read it, just about everyone who has heard of *In Search* knows at least about that "evening kiss" that the child, to his intense distress, has to forego when the parents have guests for dinner. On one particular occasion, as Charles Swann, a neighbor in Combray, a friend of the family and frequent guest (and a central character in the novel), is dining with them, the child, as usual, is sent to bed; on a particular night, however, he decides to rebel and to wait for his mother on the stair landing, even if it means facing the father's anger. However, events unfold differently.

In an act of unexpected benevolence, the father tells the mother to stay with the unhappy son. She will spend the night in the child's room; before sleep, and to calm the boy, she reads to him a novel by Georges Sand: *François le champi*. It is the story of an orphaned boy adopted by a miller and his wife, Madeleine. As the boy grows up, he falls in love with the miller's wife, who reciprocates his feelings. After being away for some years, he returns. Madeleine's husband is dead. She and the boy avow their mutual love to each other and marry.

What more convincing symbol could there have been of the bond that tied the Narrator to his mother and the mother to her son? This has been recognized by the author's biographers, but it's the child's love for the mother that is stressed (Carter, *Manuel Proust*, 24). In fact, although the Narrator built up the successive stages of that crucial episode and chose Sand's novel as a symbol for the quasi-incestuous love between mother and son, he stresses that Mamma chose the book among several other possibilities prepared by the grandmother ahead of the boy's birthday and, in reading, avoided the love sequences; in other words, she was very well aware of the story to which she was introducing her son. Isn't the Narrator pointing to the fact that the mother was, in her way, enhancing the son's emotional dependence upon her?

Some commentators have gone much further regarding the significance of *François le champi*. The miller's wife's name being Madeleine, there was but one step to identify the bliss attached to her person with the bliss produced by a madeleine, the name of the small shell-shaped cake that Aunt Léonie, the grandfather's bedridden sister, the owner of the Combray house, used to offer to the Narrator. It was of course the taste of a madeleine, dipped by Mamma in a cup of tea, tens of years later, on a cold and rainy day, that suddenly brought back to him, in a surge of involuntary memory, Combray, and all the enchantment of his childhood there. The identification has been brought even further to Mary Magdalene of the Gospels and to another Madeleine in an early story written by the author. All such identifications are possible but, in my view, somewhat far-fetched (the reference here is to Julia Kristeva, *Proust and the Sense of Time*, 40–44).

Incidentally, as we shall see in greater detail further on, it's rare that the books that the Narrator repeatedly refers to don't come with some barely hidden subtext. Thus the grandmother/mother loves to read and quotes profusely from Madame de Sévigné's *Letters* to her daughter. This correspondence, which extended over some thirty years, is one of the best-known texts of French seventeenth-century literature and a monument to a mother's love for her daughter (the first staying in Paris and the second living in Provence, where her husband exercises the function of King Louis XIV's delegate). The transposition from daughter to son is as obvious as the meaning of *François le champi*.

The Narrator's love for his mother/grandmother lasts beyond the grandmother's death, until the mother's disappearance from the story, after their voyage to Venice, close to the end of the novel. This bond may have been offered by the author as the model of deep reciprocal love amid a complex tapestry of all possible forms of unrequited, unilateral love relations: heterosexual and homosexual, sadistic, mercenary, and those that lack all feelings of the most basic human empathy.

Proust's literary descriptions of the bond between him and his mother started in his earliest writings, particularly in *Pleasures and Days*, published in 1896, and, as we saw, in *Jean Santeuil*. The description of the evening kiss appears in the first story of *Pleasures and Days*, "The Death of Baldassare Silvande," and in a remarkably vivid evocation, in the same book, in "The Confession of a Young Woman" (*Pleasures and Days*, 32, 106, et al.); some seventeen years later, readers were introduced to the Narrator's description in *Search*.

Notwithstanding such early literary renditions of the mother-son bond, it's the mother's final absence from the *Search* that is most important. Couldn't the Narrator's attitude have been induced by some love-hate triggered by his excessive emotional dependence on the mother? Moreover, according to the memoirs of Céleste Albaret, Proust's housekeeper for the last ten years of his life and his most trusted confidante, he used to go once a year to put pebbles on his maternal grandparents' grave, thus following a common Jewish tradition (Albaret, *Monsieur Proust*, 178). This act was done in spite of the fact Proust was agnostic and, as we shall see, not very positive regarding his Jewishness—a theme I shall deal with at length in the next chapter. Who could have convinced him to partake in that ritual but the mother? The author/Narrator's resentment at the mother's Jewishness may well have added one more reason to the son's mixed feelings at times.

The Narrator expresses some criticism of the mother when, for example, he alludes to her social conservatism or, more precisely, her upper-middle-class snobbishness. "My mother," the Narrator writes, "was too much my grandfather's daughter not to accept in social matters, the rule of caste. People at Combray might have kind hearts and sensitive natures, might have adopted the noblest theories of human equality, yet my mother, when a footman showed signs of forgetting his place, began to say 'you' and gradually slipped out of the habit of addressing me in the third person, was moved by these presumptions to the same wrath that breaks out in Saint-Simon's *Memoirs* whenever..." Here the Narrator gives an example from those *Memoirs* and then goes on: "She would have been as reluctant to shake hands with a footman as she was ready to give him ten francs...To her, whether she admitted it or not, masters were masters and the servants were the people who fed in the kitchen" (*Search*, IV, 579).

These astonishing few lines are revealing: first, the Narrator doesn't seem aware of the fact that referring to Saint-Simon's wrath about a nobleman's misstep in order to offer it as a valid example of his mother's anger at the missteps of her servants means alluding to social norms of the time of Louis XIV to explain her behavior, a comparison that is both grotesque and offensive. The Narrator then goes on to attribute his mother's behavior to that of her own father, a scion of Combray, whereas, in reality, Proust's mother was of Jewish-Alsatian background.

What is true and what is invented in that description of the mother's ancestry? The Narrator did a simple transposition, from his mother's generation to his grandparents' one: in the novel, it is not only the mother who married a native of Combray; it is also the grandmother. Moreover, that local grandfather, albeit not an anti-Semite, partook of the common popular suspicion of seeing a Jew hiding behind any ordinary French name; he had taken the habit of signaling the "danger" to all those who could have been fooled by humming opera tunes and saying words notoriously alluding to Jews or Jewishness.

Mainly, the Narrator can use the fiction of the mother's roots in Combray, as we just saw. Technically, he is in the clear. But this sleight of hand is ironic, as Proust's mother was apparently not very fond of her Combray (Illiers) in-laws, "not her sort, one may safely assume, nor was she theirs" (Taylor, *Proust*, 7). Moreover, even in the novel, the Narrator's construct is soon contradicted by his own description: the mother, in the text, is a copy of her own mother, the Narrator's grandmother, who is said to have come from another background and is depicted as the model of humility and goodness: "She had brought so different a type of mind into my father's family that everyone made fun of her" (*Search*, I, 13). Although the grandmother wouldn't even have been able to imagine the kind of attitude to servants attributed to the mother, it's from her that her daughter got her values, as the novel regularly shows. As we shall see in the next chapter, the Narrator offers further proofs of the mother's roots in a very different world.

It's obvious throughout the novel that the Narrator's attitude to his mother is ambiguous, whether because of her over-possessiveness or her Jewishness (over-possessiveness being a stereotype of Jewish mothers). That this ambiguity led to desecration and sadistic rituals can nowhere be proven, even if some of it could possibly be attributed to the author (Tadié, *Marcel Proust*, 672–73). I will return to this issue. Let me add that some commentators, Painter in particular, see in the Narrator's love-hatred toward the mother the axis on which the entire novel is built and the fundamental underpinning of the author's life.

In an apt allegory, the Narrator presents the last major scene in which we encounter Mamma. She has taken her son, who should be in his thirties by then, to Venice. After a few weeks, she wishes to return to Paris, while the son, who has learned of the arrival of a woman in whom he is interested, wants to stay. The mother packs her own things and also his and departs for the railway station. For a while he lingers at the hotel, determined to have his own way, but no, he cannot. At the last moment, he rushes to the station and arrives just in time to join the mother... The Narrator wants to assert himself, but he cannot bear to act against his mother's wishes. She is his jailer in a sense, but also the only permanent love of his life.

In an interesting analysis of the Venice episode, Leo Bersani interprets the Narrator's inability to withstand the short stay without his mother, while, forlorn, he listens to a musician, as an emptiness of the self, a self that desperately needs the mother's presence to feel whole again, to know that he has been forgiven. "To feel alone means, for Marcel, not only the absence of another person, but, most painfully, his own absence. He has lost his sense of himself; he is nothing more than a beating heart and an attention anxiously following the notes of *Sole mio*. It seems that he is sad not simply because he has caused his mother pain, but also because this means that his mother now has an unfavorable image of him . . . He has, in fact, always depended on her willingness to provide a certain image of himself" (Bersani, *Marcel Proust: The Fictions of Life and of Art*, 7).

What should be added, though, is the mother's inability to let her son enjoy another love. In other words, as much as the Narrator needs the exclusive attachment of the mother, so does the mother need the exclusive attachment of her son. Tug of love, tug of war.

I am not done with the mother: the next chapter will include some further traits. One crucial element should, however, be stressed at this early stage. The Narrator needs the mother's love like air for breathing, but as mentioned, resentment is increasingly present over time; the Venice allegory clearly shows it. For the grown-up Narrator the mother's possessiveness is a major hindrance, yet whatever his annoyance may have been, there is no proof that Proust was involved in any desecration rites of the mother's memory (an episode I will discuss further on). This being said, there is little doubt that the flow of the author's and Narrator's love for Mamma remains seriously hampered by contrary currents. Ultimately, for both of them only the mother's disappearance allows the temporary resolution of this conflict of feelings and the start of the great novel. It is through the writing of *In Search* that the conflict will be resolved, and the mother's love recaptured in its pristine purity.

In the case of Proust himself, what appears as a flimsy hypothesis on my part is easily tested: the mother dies at the end of September 1905 and, by 1908, the author has begun writing *Contre Sainte-Beuve,* in which many scenes of the future novel appear in imagined conversations between Marcel and his mother ("Talking to Mamma"), among other sequences. Within a few months the elements of literary criticism that are part of that hybrid essay are abandoned, and work on *In Search* fully begins.

In the Narrator's rendition, the mother has simply disappeared; he has left Paris for a longer period. On his return, he accepts an invitation to a matinee at the Princesse de Guermantes's and, in the courtyard of the sumptuous habitation, he experiences a sudden epiphany that will allow him to recapture his long-lost confidence in his ability to become a writer and begin the composition of the novel in which, from the very outset, the mother appears as the unquestioned love of his life.

However, for the Narrator, as for the author, no mixed feelings regarding Mamma will be relevant anymore: she is gone, and from now on it's writing that fulfills their lives.

TO BE OR NOT TO BE A JEW?

Proust was born of provincial French stock on his father's side (Adrien Proust was the son of a grocer from Illiers, the little town southeast of Paris that becomes Combray in the novel) and of French-Jewish descent on his mother's side (Jeanne Weill came from a wealthy Parisian family of Alsatian-Jewish background). Marcel was baptized and seen as Catholic, up to a point. Whether he defined himself as Catholic or whether he attached some importance to his Jewish background is precisely one of the questions I shall try to elucidate here, by listening to the Narrator.

The Narrator of *In Search* is not a Jew. Almost all commentators mention this evident fact and are done with the issue.

In *The Western Canon*, Harold Bloom considered it necessary to justify Proust's choice of a narrator who was neither

Jewish nor homosexual: "Proust rightly judged that the Narrator would be most effective if he could assume a dispassionate stance regarding the mythology that raises the narrative into a cosmological poem, Dantesque as well as Shakespearean. Balzac, Stendhal, Flaubert are left behind in Proust's leap into a vision that compounds Sodom and Gomorrah, Jerusalem, and Eden: three abandoned paradises. The Narrator, as a Gentile heterosexual, is more persuasive as a seer of this new mythology" (Quoted in Carter, *Proust in Love*, 95).

But as I will show, the Narrator, while going so far as trying to change his mother's identity, makes any number of contrary statements (intentional or not) that show his uncertainty and his obsession with the Jewish question in general and his own identity in particular.

Here is how Proust defined himself in an oft-quoted letter of 1896 to his acquaintance (later a friend) Comte Robert de Montesquiou, in response to the latter's rant about Jews, at the height of the Dreyfus Affair: "Dear Sir, I didn't answer yesterday to your question about the Jews. It is for a simple reason: whereas I am Catholic like my father and my brother, my mother on the other hand is Jewish. You understand that this is a strong enough reason for my abstaining from this kind of discussion. I thought that it was more respectful to write to you about it than to tell you so in the presence of another person. But I am very happy about this occasion that allows me to tell you something I possibly would never have thought of telling you. For, if our ideas differ or rather if I am not free to have on this topic those I would perhaps have, you could have involuntarily wounded me in a discussion..." (Proust, *Lettres*, 144, my translation).

The letter is ambiguous, and we don't know whether Proust's stand refers to Jewishness or to the Dreyfus Affair (to be discussed further on), what he means by "[ideas] I would perhaps have," what in it is sheer politeness and a wish to maintain good relations with the count, and what is the author's stand about partaking of his mother's Jewishness.

In the novel, the parents and young Marcel appear from the outset as pious Catholics, at least during their stay in Combray. Not only do they go to Mass every Sunday but they add to it the observance of the *mois de Marie*, a month particularly devoted to the cult of the Virgin Mary, both of which pieties indicate a religious commitment well above average. Later, neither the Narrator nor the author mention any specific religious faith or practice, except for some vague religiosity ("préoccupation religieuse") that, as Proust wrote in September 1915 to Lionel Hauser, his banker and friend, "is never absent any day of my life" (Proust, *Lettres*, 738).

From his mother's side of the family, Proust certainly got some knowledge of Jewish religious customs, such as the pebbles you put on graves, or the ashes, as mentioned by the Narrator, that "the Jews used to cover their heads in times of mourning" (*Search*, III, 539), and of some Yiddish words generally used in the parlance of Alsatian Jews and of Ashkenazi Jews more generally. The Narrator attributes, for example, to the Bloch family the use of "schlemiel," a very common

Yiddish term indicating a good-for-nothing, and also the word "meschores," meaning "servant," a word probably used in the conversation of Alsatian Jews, derived from the Hebrew *mesharet* (servant). Whether he knew more is hard to assess, as much of his references to "sensitive" topics are allusive. In the words of Antoine Compagnon, "Translators of Proust are therefore not at all misguided in assuming that there are allusions just about everywhere in the *Recherche*, but most especially with regard to Zion and Sodom" (Compagnon, "Lost Allusions in *À la recherche du temps perdu*," in *Proust in Perspective*, 146).

Incidentally, one may wonder why in Proust's early unpublished novel, *Jean Santeuil*, references to Jews are very positive (except for the crook Schlechtemburg) and in one case (that of the politician Marie's wife) dithyrambic, while, thirteen years later, in the *Search*, they become often negative. The reason seems obvious: when *Jean Santeuil* was written, between 1896 and 1899, the author's mother was alive, while when Proust started writing his great novel, she had been dead for three years.

Let me return to the mother's weird genealogical construct, a construct that convinced even as subtle a commentator as William C. Carter that the Narrator's mother was not Jewish: "The Narrator, who resembles Proust in many ways, is different in others...His mother, unlike Jeanne Proust, is not Jewish nor is the hero's father a distinguished medical luminary..." (William C. Carter, "The vast structure of recollection from life to literature," in *Cambridge*

Companion, 38). Actually, nowhere in the *Search* is the father's origin or family explicitly mentioned, and for good reason: the provincial Combray values, those of the maternal grandfather, are supposedly transmitted to the mother, as we saw. There is no place for the father's background, except if father and grandfather are considered as one and the same person. However, the Narrator's memories of those enchanted times clearly show that mother and grandmother belong to another world. And, as previously alluded to, the Narrator allowed for small indications of the mother's tight link to her own mother's background, for example when he quoted her telling young Marcel that *Empfindung* (sensibility in German) was to be distinguished from the *Empfindelei* (approximately mawkish sensibility) that at times he indulged in (*Search*, V, 135). The use of *Empfindelei* points to an excellent knowledge of colloquial German, probably rare among true natives of Combray...

The Narrator's attitude towards Jews is contradictory throughout the *Search*. On the one hand, his remarks can be neutral to positive, mainly when dealing with thoroughly assimilated Jews like Charles Swann: "Like certain other Jews, my parents' old friend had contrived to illustrate in turn all the successive stages through which those of his race had passed, from the most naïve snobbery and the crudest caddishness to the most exquisite good manners" (*Search*, II, 2). More blatantly, though, *In Search* is replete with anti-Semitic remarks adopted by the Narrator without any comment, although in part they are manifestly meant to describe the widespread anti-Semitism of different classes of French society. For instance, after the middle-class Albertine meets Albert Bloch, the Narrator's former school comrade, she exclaims after hearing his name: "I would have betted anything he was a Yid. Typical of their creepy ways!" (*Search*, II, 629). Even positive traits that the naive reader may consider as compliments, such as Bloch's intellectual prowess (he passed the *agrégation*, an extremely selective French exam) or the very close relations between members of the Bloch family, were in fact well-known anti-Semitic topoi in the Western world at the time—and later. Incidentally, an early anti-Semitic description of the appearance and mentality of Jews, attributed to Marcel by some biographers, is in fact a quote from Bouvard and Pécuchet, two notorious fictional characters created by Gustave Flaubert who voice the stupidity of French society—young Proust wrote about them in *Pleasures and Days* (77).

The paradoxical aspect of the Narrator's anti-Semitic remarks resides in the fact that Proust, who was explicit, as we saw, about the Jewishness of his mother, allows the Narrator to refer time and again to the collective racial traits of the Jews ("Jewish blood," *Search*, II, 644), thus logically including himself in that community. In fact, in an unpublished addendum to the novel, Proust demonstrates, perhaps inadvertently, and in any case metaphorically, that he believed in the commonality of essence among Jews, by describing Lady

Israels, the wife of Sir Rufus Israels, a Jewish financier, in a visit to a French aristocratic lady, and calling her first by her name and then as "Lady Jacob" (*Search*, II, 735).

More immediately visible in the Narrator's descriptions of Jews are physical characteristics commonly attributed to them. This includes the Narrator's most admired character, his family's neighbor, Charles Swann. Even though he is admitted into the most exclusive aristocratic salons, he cannot escape the Jewish hallmark, rendered more visible in his case by illness: the Jewish nose: "Swann's punchinello nose, absorbed for long years into an agreeable face, seemed now enormous, tumid, crimson, the nose of an old Hebrew rather than that of a dilettante Valois. Perhaps, too, in these last days, the physical type that characterises his race was becoming more pronounced in him, at the same time as a sense of moral solidarity with the rest of the Jews, a solidarity which Swann seemed to have forgotten throughout his life, and which, one after another, his mortal illness, the Dreyfus case and the anti-semitic propaganda had reawakened" (*Search*, IV, 121–22).

In fact, although the comments about Jews in the *Search* are more often negative than favorable, favorable descriptions appear as well, sometimes quite emphatically: "Generally speaking, one realised . . . that, if it could be held against [the Jews] that their hair was too long, their noses and eyes were too big, their gestures abrupt and theatrical, it was puerile to judge them by this, that they had plenty of wit and good-heartedness, and were men to whom, in the long run, one could become closely attached. Among the Jews especially there were few whose parents and kinsfolk had not a warmth of heart, a breadth of mind, a sincerity, in comparison with which Saint-Loup's mother [Madame de Marsantes, the mother of the Narrator's aristocratic friend] and the Duc de Guermantes [one of the top figures of the Faubourg Saint-Germain, the area of Paris supposedly inhabited by the highest French aristocracy] cut the poorest of moral figures by their aridity, their skin-deep religiosity which denounced only the most open scandal, their apology for a Christianity which led invariably... to a colossally mercenary marriage" (*Search*, III, 559–60).

The author himself seemed truly worried by the widespread anti-Semitism in French society, as appears from a letter of July 1903 to his friend Georges de Lauris (Proust, *Lettres*, 244–45). In short, we witness a constant seesaw in the Narrator's attitude toward Jews, and no less so in that of the author. The Dreyfus Affair became the formidable accelerator of attitudes toward Jews, but also, very soon, an essentially political struggle that rent France into two violently hostile camps, irrespective of the Jewish issue.

In the 1880s and the early '90s, endemic French anti-Semitism was exacerbated by several major scandals in which prominent Jews played some roles: the crash of a Catholic bank, the Union Générale, which was blamed on the Banque Rothschild, and, mainly, the so-called Panama Scandal. These occurred when the Panama Company, presided over by Ferdinand de Lesseps, who had built the Suez Canal, failed in 1892 in its attempt to build the American equivalent. As many French political figures had financial interests in the enterprise, the company distributed massive bribes in an attempt to hide the failure from the wider public. The main agents in the bribing operation were two Jews of German background, Baron Jacques de Reinach and Cornelius Herz. Before he committed suicide, Reinach gave the list of the public figures involved to Edouard Drumont, the publisher of the anti-Semitic paper *La libre parole*, in hopes of covering himself.

Drumont was the author of the rabidly anti-Jewish pamphlet *La France juive*. Published in 1885, it became a runaway best seller, bolstered in its aggressive anti-Jewish incitement by *La libre parole*, which was made instantly famous by Reinach's list.

It was in that poisonous atmosphere that a Jewish artillery officer, Captain Alfred Dreyfus, was arrested in 1894 and charged with espionage on behalf of Germany; the evidence was a document later shown to be a forgery. Dreyfus was summarily tried by a military tribunal, publicly demoted, and sent to Devil's Island, part of French Guiana. Within two years, though, a campaign aiming to prove his innocence spread. As mentioned above, the country was divided into two camps: the advocates of Dreyfus's innocence (the Dreyfusards) and those convinced of his guilt (the anti-Dreyfusards). The first were mostly Jews, republicans, socialists and essentially secular; their enemies were, generally speaking, closely allied to the Catholic Church, to the army and to anti-republican, monarchist, and far-right-wing political movements. The Affair lingered well into the early years of the new century in successive stages, ultimately leading to Dreyfus's rehabilitation. Incidentally, as the Affair was essentially political, some staunch believers in Dreyfus's innocence were also dyed-in-the wool anti-Semites (as in the novel, both Madame Verdurin and Madame Sazerat were) but these were exceptions.

Marcel was openly pro-Dreyfus, and so was his brother, although, as we saw, he expressed himself strangely in his letter to Montesquiou. Their father was anti-Dreyfusard and refused to speak to his sons for two weeks after learning of their opinions. But what of the Narrator?

The Narrator declares himself pro-Dreyfus and tells us that his father, convinced that Dreyfus was guilty, refused to speak to him for a week upon learning what he thought (*Search*, III, 200). This was indeed Dr. Proust's attitude toward Marcel and his brother. It shows once more how closely the novel follows the author's biography. Regarding the Narrator's attitude in the Affair, knowing what we know of Proust's attitude toward his own Jewishness, we must agree with Jean Recanati: Proust, as the Narrator, is pro-Dreyfus because of the injustice done to the officer, because of his suffering, not because of Dreyfus's Jewishness (Recanati, *Profils juifs de Marcel Proust*, 72–73).

The Narrator explains the details of his choice by attributing them to the two Jewish figures we already met: Charles Swann and Albert Bloch. Swann encounters deeply ingrained anti-Semitism in the aristocratic milieu that has adopted him. Hostile opinions about Jews swirl around him but do not turn into personal ostracism. In fact, the Narrator intimates that while anti-Jewish opinions are frequent in mid-level aristocracy, they are less shrill, sometimes even abandoned, although generally deeply rooted, by some members of its highest ranks. Thus the Princesse des Laumes (the future Duchess de Guermantes and wife of the duke) makes fun of Mme de Gallardon's anti-Jewish remarks by reminding her that she, Mme de Gallardon, has attempted a hundred times to invite Swann, who has always refused. Later on, during the Affair, the duchess will not adopt the fierce anti-Jewish feelings of her husband, although we are told this is more because she wants to assert herself than out of any personal belief. The Duc de Guermantes, and his brother, the Baron de Charlus, both fierce anti-Semites, express the opinion of the majority.

Outwardly the entire Faubourg (with the initial exception of the Narrator's friend, the eccentric Saint-Loup), believed in Dreyfus's culpability. Privately, however, the Prince de Guermantes (the duke's cousin) and his wife were soon convinced of his innocence but didn't dare admit their views, even to each other. The Narrator mentions humorously that both of them had their confessor, Abbé Poiret, who was also secretly convinced of Dreyfus's innocence, say Mass for the Jewish exile.

The duke would not relent, however, even when proofs of Dreyfus's innocence accumulated and it seemed highly probable that the verdict would be overturned. In one of the duke's multiple anti-Jewish outbursts quoted by the Narrator, he takes aim at the Rothschilds: "Of course, [the Rothschilds], even if they have the tact never to speak of that abominable affair, are Dreyfusards at heart, like all the Jews...If a Frenchman robs or murders somebody, I don't consider myself bound, because he's a Frenchman like myself, to find him innocent. But the Jews will never admit that one of their co-citizens is a traitor, although they know it perfectly well, and never think of the terrible repercussions..." (*Search*, V, 45).

It is the Narrator's longtime school comrade Bloch who is hit by the full brunt of aristocratic anti-Semitism and anti-Dreyfusard hatred in the course of a reception at the Marquise de Villeparisis's to which he was invited: he expresses his views somewhat crudely, as is his wont. Swann, who becomes increasingly explicit about his pro-Dreyfus attitude, is not ostracized, because of his decades-long friendship with the Guermantes, but he is an exception. All in all, the Narrator's position in the Affair, as expressed by Bloch and Swann, is not a conclusive indication of his feelings regarding Jews and Jewishness, as the whole Affair becomes a vast confrontation of political opinions, many of which are independent of attitudes regarding the Jews.

It is not clear whether the Narrator approves of Jews shedding their Jewishness, and one doesn't know what Proust thought of it. He may have approved, as—to a point—this was his own situation. Yet the Narrator is sarcastic about the two major examples he offers, that of Gilberte Swann (Swann's daughter) and that of Bloch. Gilberte, the Narrator's first love, reappears in the novel as Mademoiselle de Forcheville, having been adopted by Odette Swann's second husband, after Swann's death. Soon she would present herself as G. S. Forcheville: "The real hypocrisy in this signature was made manifest by the suppression not so much of the other letters of the name 'Swann' as of those of the name 'Gilberte.' For, by reducing the innocent Christian name to a simple 'G,' Mlle de Forcheville seemed to insinuate to her friends that the similar amputation applied to the name 'Swann' was due equally to the necessity of abbreviation. Indeed she gave a special significance to the 'S,' extending it with a sort of long tail which ran across the 'G,' but which one felt to be transitory and destined to disappear like the tail which, still long in the monkey, has ceased to exist in man" (*Search*, V, 793).

The Narrator describes without comment the mutation, later in life, of his school friend Bloch, who changes his very Jewish name to Jacques du Rozier and his appearance to that of an English dandy, "beneath which it would have needed my grandfather's flair to detect 'the sweet vale of Hebron' and those 'chains of Israel' which my old schoolmate seemed definitively to have broken." (*Search*, VI, 384).

Approves or not? Actually one doesn't need grandpa's flair, due to the Narrator's sly intimation that no external change can ultimately hide a Jewish origin: Bloch's new name carries its prior identity barely under the surface, "du Rozier" remaining very close to rue "des Rosiers," the best-known street in the traditionally Jewish area of Paris (Raczymow, *Le Cygne,* 39). The Narrator seems to be saying that whatever you do to hide your Jewish origin, it will remain visible and soon recognized. To make his point even clearer, the Narrator also insists on Jewish physical characteristics that, even if they weren't too visible in midlife, reappear with old age and illness, as we saw regarding Swann.

The author's view about such attempts to hide one's origins is opaque for a further reason: in the case of both Gilberte and Bloch, the Narrator, without having to stress it, describes their attempts with heavy irony, but is also certainly aware of his own hesitations regarding self-presentation.

The social identification of Jews may have been particularly true in France during the Affair and its immediate aftermath. Open anti-Semitism decreased, however, during the Great War, even in previously shrill anti-Jewish political parties such as the Action Française or among notorious anti-Semitic writers such as Maurice Barrès. During the late war period and the immediate postwar years, the Bolshevik Revolution and, slightly thereafter, the publication of *The Protocols of the Elders of Zion* triggered a new wave of anti-Jewish feeling. In the early twenties, Proust, already very ill, concentrated essentially on finishing his novel and probably didn't follow the ups and downs of his country's anti-Jewish hostility. He died in 1922.

There is a sentence in *Time Regained* that simply cannot be integrated in the litany of unpleasant remarks that the Narrator makes about Bloch's Jewish physical and moral characteristics, a theme that recurs an unusual number of times in the description of a matinee at the Princesse de Guermantes's. (This is the last and most important such occasion in the novel, as the Narrator, who has returned to Paris after a long absence, suddenly discovers, to his amazement, the impact of time on the people he knew—and upon himself.) Thus, after several Bloch-related comments, the Narrator, without any other immediate context, declares: "Bloch had come bounding into the room like a hyena" (*Search*, VI, 406). Like a hyena? There are few animals more disgusting than hyenas in common parlance; they are perceived as scavengers, feeding on carrion. But "bounding"? Hyenas are not known for bounding in any special way. The use of this unusual comparison to describe a person entering a room can only mean pushing oneself, entering by force or something similar. "Bounding like a hyena" makes no sense, except that it indicates the Narrator's wish to be as insulting as possible . . . toward an old friend.

The appellation was not haphazard; the Narrator had used the same insulting metaphor to describe Bloch's arrival, about twenty years earlier, to the reception at the Marquise de Villeparisis's: "the Romanians, the Egyptians, the Turks may hate the Jews. But in a French drawing-room the differences between those peoples are not so apparent, and a Jew making his entry as though he were emerging from the desert, his body crouching like a hyena's, his neck thrust forward, offering profound 'salaams,' completely satisfies a certain taste for the oriental" (*Search*, III, 253). In the previous quote, Bloch-the-hyena was bounding; now he is crouching; in both cases he reminds us of pest-carrying rats. And yet, in both cases, after hurling these obnoxious insults, the Narrator returns to almost friendly remarks about his Jewish childhood friend, as if the hyena had never been mentioned...

One may remember that in his answer to Montesquiou's anti-Jewish rant of 1896, Proust indicates that given the Jewishness of his mother he cannot express thoughts that he might have had otherwise. Now, as he completes *In Search*, the author need not bother about his mother anymore, dead since 1905: Bloch could crouch like a hyena or bounce into the room like a hyena; nobody would object, not even the Jews.

I shall attempt now to get a better perspective by concentrating on what are, to my mind, the most extraordinary constructs indulged in by the Narrator: the mother's strange genealogy and the use of "hyena" to describe Bloch on two occasions. Both constructs escaped the attention of an otherwise very subtle and attentive interpreter of Proust's writings about Jews, Jean Recanati. In an essay on the subject,

Recanati, who incidentally put more emphasis on *Jean Santeuil* than on *In Search*, made an important point that is valid for all of Proust's writings on the topic. The Narrator, particularly in the great novel, creates a dichotomy between the moral and physical characteristics of French higher classes and those of Jews (Recanati, *Profils juifs de Marcel Proust*). This dichotomy, from which even Swann did not escape, becomes paradigmatic, let us say, in the figures of Saint-Loup and Bloch.

The genealogy that the Narrator establishes for his mother clearly appears as some sort of redemption, a redemption from her Jewishness. It attributes to her a rootedness in true France (*"le pays réel,"* as Charles Maurras, the founder of the Action Française, would say, opposing it to *"le pays légal"* of the Jews) and moreover attributes to her a particularly strict code of behavior toward her servants, one that would have been acceptable to the Duc de Saint-Simon as fitting Louis XIV's court.

The Narrator's vagaries lead us to a further detail that was mentioned in the previous chapter, still not explained. I wondered at the absence of all physical description of the Narrator's parents but left the issue unresolved. Now, in light of the attempt to turn the mother into a "child of Combray," the reason for such avoidance seems clear: the mother looked Jewish, or, more precisely, she must have looked Jewish in the eyes of the author. Of course, Proust could have allowed the Narrator to describe her as Combray-like, but we may guess that remnants of that filial love so movingly described in the novel and so real for the author didn't allow the Narrator to go that far. And probably for the same general reason, the parents' names are nowhere mentioned. The Narrator could not give the mother a maiden name such as "Dupont" or "Durand" (both common French surnames) and couldn't give a French last name to the father alone.

Bloch's figure is related to this weird semi-attempt to redeem the mother from her Jewishness. He is as brash as she is delicate, as uncouth as her displays of perfect manners, as hyena-like as she may be...an imagined aristocrat. There is the rub, in the Narrator's contradictions.

On one hand, the Narrator wants to redeem the mother, on the other hand he points indirectly to her Jewishness. Almost from the outset of the novel he tells us that the grandmother brings to the Combray milieu values that derive from an entirely different background (a Jewish one, of course). On the same occasion, he cannot hide his admiration for the upright yet humble, forgiving, and loving Bathilde (the grandmother's first name). And throughout the novel, the mutual love and devotion between mother and grandmother are a recurrent theme. The grandmother's generosity and kindness could not have generated the mother's severe code of behavior toward her servants. Moreover, as we saw previously, *Empfindelei* demonstrates clearly enough that the mother is worlds away from any Combray ascendance.

The Narrator's equivocations about his mother's representation are just one aspect of Proust's indecision regarding his own Jewishness, and Jews more generally. If we accept the dichotomy suggested by Recanati—and as I mentioned it looked convincing to me—then we have to follow him one step further. In much of Proust's fiction, the pure French often display physical characteristics such as blond hair and an erect gait. At that point the author sometimes adds Jewish characteristics to them, as in *Jean Santeuil*, when he describes Colonel Picquart's entrance into the courtroom, in one of the judicial sequels of the Dreyfus Affair, that he looked like an "Israelite engineer" (Recanati, *Profils Juifs de Marcel Proust*, 82).

Actually such mixing of characteristics that, in principle, belong to opposite entities, appears so often in *Search* (and not only in Swann's hair color) as to suggest that it is intentional. Why, for example, does the Narrator feel the need to describe the Duchesse de Guermantes with an arched nose (*Search*, III, 63)? And why, in the affair between Saint-Loup and his Jewish mistress Rachel, does Saint-Loup look like the cad in trying to get her back by promising a sumptuous necklace as reward, a reward that she, the Jewess, rejects?

Swann and two of his real-life models, the French Jew Charles Haas and of course Marcel Proust himself, all considered themselves accepted by the Faubourg (see Raczymow, *Le cygne*, for more about Haas). The Narrator ultimately has some doubts about that acceptance, though: when Swann lets her know that he is terminally ill, the Duchesse de Guermantes shows greater interest in the shoes she has to wear than in the tragic situation of her closest friend for many years.

It seems that Narrator (and author) remain undecided to the end on how to relate to Jewishness, specifically that of Swann and Bloch. I would suggest, at this stage at least, that the Narrator's resentment against Jews was neither ideological nor political. It was social. The Narrator cannot bear seeing Jews from a lower social situation than his climbing furiously to the position that he thinks he has achieved. He explains it quite clearly regarding his school comrade: "Bloch was ill-bred, neurotic and snobbish, and since he belonged to a family of little repute, had to support, as on the floor of the ocean, the incalculable pressures imposed on him not only by the Christians at the surface but by all the intervening layers of Jewish castes superior to his own, each of them crushing with its contempt the one that was immediately beneath it . . ." (*Search*, II, 442).

At the Princesse de Guermantes's last reception, the Narrator cannot but recognize Bloch's social ascension: hence, in part, his fury. The words that follow his outburst say it all: "In ten years, in drawing-rooms like this which their own feebleness of spirit would allow [Bloch] to dominate, he would enter on crutches to be greeted as 'the Master' for whom a visit to the [noble family] La Trémoïlles was merely a tedious obligation. And what would this profit him?" (*Search*, VI, 407). The Narrator couldn't let go of the last sentence, the parting shot . . . I will return to it.

.3.

FORBIDDEN LOVE

I n his eloquent defense of homosexuality in the opening pages of *Sodom and Gomorrah*, the Narrator compares the fate of the invert with that of the Jew: both are compelled by social conventions to hide their true nature. The fate of both groups is similar as far as being pariahs is concerned, but while the Jews, even if rejected by many, do not, and rarely can, hide their Jewishness, inverts usually cannot, except among themselves, openly admit their sexual preferences.

In the words of the Narrator, the inverts are a "race upon which a curse is laid and which must live in falsehood and perjury because it knows that its desire, that which constitutes life's dearest pleasure, is held to be punishable, shameful, an inadmissible thing... sons without a mother, to whom they are obliged to lie even in the hour when they close her dying eyes; friends without friendships, despite all those which their frequently acknowledged charm inspires and their often generous hearts would gladly feel—but can we describe as friendships those relationships which flourish only by virtue of a lie ...?" (*Search*, IV, 20).

Yet notwithstanding his defense, the Narrator strangely contradicts himself at some point in his portrayal of the male invert, as we shall see. But, while the Narrator did not know how to handle the part-Jewishness he was unavoidably carrying in himself, he never, throughout *In Search*, admits to even a whiff of homosexuality. On the contrary, we witness the blossoming of his heterosexual love life, from his love for Gilberte Swann, to his infatuation with the Duchesse de Guermantes, and to his major affair with Albertine. There may be involuntary hints, of course, at his true nature.

For instance, it's clear that the Narrator admires handsome males. He reminisces, for example, about his first sight of Saint-Loup at Balbec: "Because of his 'tone,' because he had the insolent manner of a young 'blood,' above all because of his extraordinary good looks, some even thought him effeminate-looking, though without holding it against him since they knew how virile he was and how passionately fond of women" (*Search*, II, 421). Saint-Loup, as becomes apparent toward the end of the novel, is bisexual. The only entirely homosexual character is Charlus, whose looks the Narrator doesn't miss: "I looked at M. de Charlus. Undoubtedly his magnificent head, though repellent [because of a momentary rage], yet far surpassed that of any of his relatives; he was like an ageing Apollo..." (*Search*, III, 761).

As a foil for his visions of male beauty, the Narrator uses marginal snippets of physical ugliness, mainly in representations of old age, illness, and death—and of some Jewish characters...One of the most telling of those snippets shortly precedes the presentation of the entire array of *vieillards* (strangely, no equivalent exists in English, except for "the elderly") at the Princesse de Guermantes's matinee; it is the briefly mentioned meeting with Charlus on the Champs-Elysées. The Narrator is in a cab on his way to the matinee when he notices the passenger in another cab, which is about to stop: "A man with staring eyes and hunched figure was placed rather than seated in the back, and was making, to keep himself upright, the efforts that might have been made by a child who has been told to be good. But his straw hat failed to conceal an unruly forest of hair which was entirely white, and a white beard, like those which snow forms on the statues of river-gods in public gardens, flowed from his chin. It was—side by side with Jupien [whom we shall very shortly meet again], who was unremitting in his attentions to him—M. de Charlus, now convalescent after an attack of apoplexy of which I had had no knowledge" (*Search*, VI, 244–45).

At the sight of Charlus, the Narrator evokes King Lear and adds a significant detail: "But what was most moving was that one felt that this lost brightness [of Charlus's eyes] was identical with his moral pride, and that somehow the physical and even the intellectual life of M. de Charlus had survived the eclipse of that aristocratic haughtiness which had in the past seemed indissolubly linked to them" (*Search*, VI, 245). Thus, somehow, the Narrator couldn't let go of Charlus's bygone personality and even of his physical appearance. And let us remember, Charlus is the dominant personality of the second half of the novel.

Of course, Saint-Loup, the most resplendent and handsome of the younger aristocrats, had to join the other male inverts: one sensed his true nature throughout the novel, but one couldn't be sure of it until the very end, just before a heroic death at the front sealed his fate. For the Narrator, male physical beauty implies some form of splendor of the entire personality. Inversion is also linked to the right moral stance. Thus, while the gross Duc de Guermantes, an inveterate womanizer, is violently anti-Dreyfus, his cousin, the Prince de Guermantes, an invert, soon recognizes Dreyfus's innocence and, as we saw, asks his confessor to say Mass for the prisoner in Devil's Island. Of course, one cannot push this too far, as the baron's politics are not to be commended...

In depicting Charlus, the Narrator insists on stressing that under the baron's pretense of virility lies a his deeply feminine and soft-hearted personality. This aspect is quasi-central to Charlus's figure, so much so that the author even insists on it in a letter of June 1914 to André Gide: "I attempted to paint the homosexual in love with virility because, without knowing it, he is a woman" (*Lettres*, 690). "According to Gide," writes Carter, "Proust felt compelled, in a conversation years later, in the spring of 1921, to justify

FORBIDDEN LOVE

the absence from *Sodom and Gomorrah* of handsome, virile homosexuals like those to be idealized by Gide in *Corydon*. He confessed that in order to depict the attractive pictures of the girls in Balbec, he had drawn upon memories of his own homosexual experience. Since he had given all the young men's tender, graceful, and charming attributes to the girls in his book, there remained nothing for his homosexual portraits but 'mean and grotesque qualities'" (Carter, *Proust in Love*, 98). This explanation is strange if we consider Charlus's portrait and that of Saint-Loup. What Proust may have explained to Gide applied to the feminine aspect of his homosexual characters and not to their being depicted with "mean and grotesque qualities."

Incidentally, the Narrator's comparison between the fate of two pariah groups in French society, the homosexuals and the Jews, although obvious as such, may have been bolstered by a best-selling book, *Sex and Character*, translated into French in 1912 and penned by the Austrian (and Jewish) writer, Otto Weininger, who compared Jews to women and to homosexuals. It is likely that Proust knew at least of Weininger's main theme, widely commented on all over Europe.

Up to this point, one could suggest that the Narrator, although not in any conscious way attracted to homosexuality, defended and even admired at times inverts in general and Charlus's looks and intellect in particular. What then should we make of the fierce rant that he unleashes when he sees the baron approaching him and Professor Brichot as they are about to enter the Verdurins' Parisian house for dinner? After comparing Charlus to a Great Inquisitor painted by El Greco, the Narrator goes on: "But this priest was frightening and looked like an excommunicate, the various compromises to which he had been driven by the need to indulge his taste and to keep it secret having had the effect of bringing to the surface of his face precisely what the Baron sought to conceal, a debauched life betrayed by moral degeneration. This last, indeed, whatever be its cause, is easily detected, for it is never slow to materialise and proliferates upon a face, especially on the cheeks and round the eyes, as physically as the ochreous yellows of jaundice or the repulsive reds of a skin disease. Nor was it merely in the cheeks, or rather the chaps, of this painted face, in the mammiferous chest, the fleshy rump of this body abandoned to self-indulgence and invaded by obesity, that there now lingered, spreading like a film of oil, the vice at one time so jealously confined by M. de Charlus in the most secret recesses of his being. Now it overflowed into his speech" (*Search*, V, 272–73).

What should we make of this? How can we reconcile it with the eloquent defense of homosexuality we quoted beforehand? This is the language of hatred. Was the author pandering to the vast readership that he expected after receiving the Goncourt Prize in 1919 (the volume from which I now quoted—*The Captive & The Fugitive*—was published posthumously)? Is that the only available explanation? This specific problem is part of an apparently wider inconsistency regarding homosexuality in the novel.

Although the Narrator presents himself as thoroughly heterosexual, in *Jean Santeuil*, a text that Proust meant to be a barely altered autobiography, Jean's homosexuality is strongly hinted at (although never mentioned as such) in the story of his intense, mutually shared, teenage friendship with Henri de Réveillon (a one-page female episode, thoroughly unconvincing, is thrown in, and rather confirms the homosexual feelings of the two young men). In fact, in that story Proust describes his first great love affair with the young composer Reynaldo Hahn; even the names of the sites to which they traveled together are the same in the novel as they were in reality. The novel remained unpublished for decades but as far as we know that was due to the author's own dissatisfaction with its literary quality and not because of any moral qualms.

Proust did hide some stories, initially meant to be included in *Les plaisirs et les jours*. They were found in the 1950s but published only very recently (2019). They mostly deal quite explicitly with the homosexual passions of their narrators, sometimes females, at times males. But these revealing stories were written in the 1890s by a very young author and, even before *Jean Santeuil*, a novel initially intended for publication, as just mentioned. Thus, the hiding of these few stories does not say much about the Narrator's paradoxical handling of homosexuality in the *Search*, that is some fifteen to twenty years later at least. (For these stories and the comments of their editor, see Luc Fraisse, ed., Marcel Proust, *Le mystérieux correspondant et autres nouvelles inédites*.)

In *Contre Sainte-Beuve*, chapter 13, entitled "A race accursed," the author, in describing the homosexual Comte de Quercy, uses many of the arguments that will reappear, sometimes verbatim, in his defense of homosexuality at the opening of *Sodom and Gomorrah* (*Marcel Proust on Art and Literature*, 210 and following); the volume was initially meant to be published. It indicates that Proust was ready to flaunt his homosexuality, even in writing. In any case, although in *Sodom and Gomorrah* the Narrator remains heterosexual, as he does throughout *In Search*, and doesn't spring on us a surprise à la Saint-Loup, many readers may have guessed his true inclination.

Moreover, in his social life, Proust did not hide his sexual preferences; his relations with Reynaldo Hahn or with Lucien Daudet were not kept secret, nor was his infatuation with Bertrand de Fénelon. He told quite a few people about his unrequited and tragic love for Alfred Agostinelli, a young man whom Proust first hired as car driver, then as secretary, and who was killed in early 1914, when the plane he was piloting crashed in the sea. And even if Proust was more secretive about his nocturnal expeditions during the war, his reputation was well established by then.

In his correspondence with Montesquiou, Proust was more than open, and he was the same in his letters and conversations with Gide. Thus—and this is the issue—why such a sudden contradictory attitude in the rant against Charlus in the *Search*? As I suggested above, Proust may have surmised that an openly homosexual novel, without any disclaimer, would have repelled many readers. Is that the answer? I do not know.

A mirroring of moments of love and pain in the *Search* may be a minor interpretation for the choice of heterosexuality by the Narrator, on top of the worry about readers' reactions and apart from Harold Bloom's grand interpretation. The love for the mother and the pain she caused was the root in the novel of all other such episodes, ending up with a quasi-identical scene during the love affair with Albertine. The Narrator himself leads us in that direction: "I was only too happy, as afternoon turned to evening, that the hour was not far off when I should be able to look to Albertine's presence for the appeasement which I needed. Unfortunately, the evening that followed was one of those when this appeasement was not forthcoming, when the kiss that Albertine would give me when she left me for the night, very different from her usual kiss, would no more soothe me than my mother's kiss had soothed me long ago, on days she was vexed with me and I dared not call her back although I knew I should be unable to sleep" (*Search*, V, 107–108). The Narrator insists several times on that resemblance in *The Captive*. If the mother was the matrix of a chain of mirroring moments of love and pain, these could not, at least in the novel, be enacted by males.

No wonder that Albertine's kiss did not soothe the Narrator...We know very little about her physicality, except that we learn, soon enough, that she is a lesbian who, at least with the Narrator, could also fill the role of a heterosexual lover; in short, like Saint-Loup, she was bisexual. But while Saint-Loup is overwhelmingly present and the baron is even more so, the reader never gets a clear physical image of Albertine; we hear her speaking and lying, we know when she comes and goes, but how does she look, naked or dressed, in lovemaking or at repose? Of course, we get tiny details here and there, mainly of Albertine asleep (her hair widely spread on the pillow), but that is all. We feel that the Narrator would like to tell us more, and at some point he describes her breasts and her vagina, but, somehow, when he does so, it sounds totally artificial, as if copied from an encyclopedia.

One cannot but agree with the assessment of the writer and diplomat Paul Morand, who knew Proust very well. He also felt that Albertine and the group of girls that the Narrator meets in Balbec are all boys in disguise. And Carter, quoting Morand, adds "that anyone who knows women at all will see immediately 'how false everything is in Proust's girls from Albertine to Andrée'" (Carter, *Proust in Love*, 101). (Incidentally, Morand was another of Proust's notoriously anti-Semitic friends.)

How different is the scene described by the hidden Narrator of the first meeting between Charlus and the tailor Jupien, whose shop opened onto the courtyard of the building where the Narrator's family had bought an apartment and where the

Duc and Duchesse de Guermantes, as well as the Marquise
de Villeparisis, owned their regal Parisian homes. The baron,
contrarily to his habits, came to pay a visit to the marquise,
who was suffering from an indisposition. It was on an early afternoon, and by pure chance the courtyard was empty. As the
baron was leaving, the tailor Jupien walked out of his shop.

Careful not to be seen, the Narrator observes the unexpected encounter. "For what did I see!" The Narrator writes:
"Face to face, in that courtyard where they had certainly
never met before...the Baron, having suddenly opened wide
his half-shut eyes, was gazing with extraordinary attentive-
ness at the ex tailor poised on the threshold of his shop, while
the latter, rooted suddenly to the spot in front of M. de Charlus, implanted there like a tree, contemplated with a look of
wonderment the plump form of the ageing Baron."

The text continues in the same vein, with a description of the changing postures of both protagonists in some
sort of silent ballet: "M. de Charlus's pose having altered,
Jupien's, as though in obedience to the laws of an occult art,
at once brought itself into harmony with it. The Baron, who
now sought to disguise the impression that had been made
on him, and yet, in spite of his affectation of indifference,
seemed unable to move away without regret, came and
went, looked vaguely into the distance in the way which
he felt would most enhance the beauty of his eyes, assumed
a smug, nonchalant, fatuous air." It leads to Jupien's own
transformation and to the Narrator's comment: "This scene
was not, however, positively comic; it was stamped with a

strangeness, or if you like a naturalness, the beauty of which steadily increased" (*Search*, IV, 5–6).

The key word in the Narrator's comment is "naturalness." The Narrator is as much at ease as the protagonists are natural; he describes something that he knows well, that pleases him, that will lead on to even further openness, leaving any scene with Albertine far behind, in a frozen artificiality. In other words, the Narrator hints to us what he avoids telling explicitly at all costs: he is "one of them," an expression that had the baron constantly worried that his secret had somehow been discovered.

A few snippets of the Narrator's lines that follow nail the message incontrovertibly: "the beauty of the reciprocal glances of M. de Charlus and Jupien arose precisely from the fact that they did not, for the moment at least, seem to be intended to lead to anything further. It was the first time I had seen the manifestation of this beauty in the Baron and Jupien... Whatever the point might be that held the M. de Charlus and the ex-tailor thus arrested, their pact seemed concluded and these superfluous glances to be but ritual preliminaries" (*Search*, IV, 7).

Jupien leaves the courtyard, the baron follows him; they both return. The baron, "deciding to precipitate matters, asked the tailor for a light, but at once observed: 'I ask you for a light, but I see I've left my cigars at home'. The laws of hospitality prevailed over the rules of coquetry. 'Come inside, you shall have everything you wish,' said the tailor, on whose features disdain now gave place to joy. The door of the shop closed behind them" (*Search*, IV, 8–9).

The Narrator hears the sounds of the lovers' frolics from behind a wall, and about half an hour later sees them again and follows their conversation outside of the shop. There, the baron, inaudible at that point to the Narrator, asks apparently for another round. Jupien, "with the supremely blissful air of a person whose self-esteem has just been profoundly flattered, and, deciding to grant M. de Charlus the favour that he had just asked of him, after various remarks lacking in refinement such as 'What a big bum you have!', said to the Baron with an air at once smiling, moved, superior and grateful: 'All right, you big baby, come along!'" (*Search*, IV, 13).

The Narrator's obvious pleasure at describing the Charlus–Jupien scene, the stark difference with the episodes of Albertine's lovemaking, all of that allows us to assume that the Narrator wanted some readers to know about the author's sexual preferences; it doesn't solve the riddle of the contradiction between so many positive (to say the least) descriptions of inversion that we mentioned and the hateful rant against the baron and the effects of his giving in to his sexual desire, also quoted above. The only interpretation that comes to my mind, and I know how flimsy it is, would be that of a belated attempt to offer a small sop to a conventional readership.

Had Proust written the volume in which the antihomosexual rant appears in the 1890s, at the time of *Jean Santeuil*, the hateful description of Charlus would possibly not have been included. The fin de siècle years in France were awash, among the middle class and the aristocracy, with a sense of decadence, a "nostalgia for mud" (*nostalgie de la boue*), a delight in inversion, obscenity, mysticism, Satanism, and the like (see, in particular Eugen Weber, *France, fin de siècle*). The years that immediately followed the end of the Great War became known somewhat later as the *années folles*, the mad years, but in victorious France, the feeling of decadence disappeared, for a while at least, and the exuberance of the mad years did not carry the morbidity of the fin de siècle. It is probable that this changed atmosphere, also carrying in vast segments of the population the memory of the immense sacrifices of war, did incite the author to assuage, be it briefly, his future readership.

This hypothesis may be reinforced by the fact that quite a few people expressed their discontent about the attribution of the 1919 Goncourt Prize to Proust instead of the other candidate, Roland Dorgelès, for his novel *Les croix de bois* (*Wooden Crosses*), a novel about the war. If we come to think about the author's personality, provocation was not one of his attributes: the implicit and explicit praise of homosexuality in the novel may have been the most that could be dared, but even so, not without some antidote.

.4.

A COMPREHENSIVE
MORAL ACCOUNTING?

The Narrator's tacit dismissal of his part-Jewish identity
was of course a legitimate choice. It nonetheless raises
the question of what values, for him (and for the author),
he may not have been able to just jettison. Were there any
such moral stances? Did they exist at all, and did they find
their expression in one way or another in the novel? It has
been common to argue that Proust's work was uniquely and
solely devoted to the cult of Literature and Art, as it fitted
the aesthetic ideals of European society at the beginning
of the twentieth century, until its cataclysmic end with the
outbreak of the world war. Yet some biographers suggest
otherwise.

"Proust's *In Search of Lost Time* [is] a vast sorting out,"
writes Benjamin Taylor, "a moral accounting as comprehen-
sive as Dante's in *The Divine Comedy*. The whole moral scale

is present, from Charlie Morel—who is, among other things, a rapist [only in words, it seems]—to the only character in those pages who is without sin and an absolute: Bathilde, the Narrator's grandmother. In *Axel's Castle* Edmund Wilson calls her the moral equivalent of the speed of light: nothing beyond Grand'mère, nothing to compare to her. Our hero must journey, like the rest of us, from selfishness to selfishness, vanity to vanity, delusion to delusion. But one cannot imagine Grand'mère having been selfish, vain, or deluded at any age. She is love, she is naturalness, she is unfallenness. When she goes, a radiance is snatched from the world. Nothing is ever the same again" (Taylor, *Proust*, 21).

The moral canvas presented in the *Search* appears, briefly, to reflect some of Proust's own values. Thus, as a result of the Dreyfus Affair, he seems to have discovered the existence of Evil, as he expressed it, in February 1896 in a letter to his friend Léon Daudet, quoted by Carter, thanking Daudet for a novel he had sent him. There he stated that although he previously had not believed in evil, he now believed in it due to the experience of it he had had in the Affair. "Now he grasped for the first time, he told Léon, many of Balzac's, Shakespeare's, and Goethe's characters who incarnate evil. Marcel was strikingly candid in using the principal culprits in the Dreyfus case to epitomize evil in a letter to Daudet, who [himself and his family] shared all the prejudices and hatreds of those men and who saw them first as heroes and, at worst, as victims of an international Jewish conspiracy. The bond of friendship that bound Marcel and Léon was impervious to the tensions of their radically opposed political and racial views." (Carter, *Marcel Proust*, 263).

How indeed should one interpret Proust's weird eulogy on the death of the father of that clan, the notoriously anti-Semitic Alphonse Daudet (*Marcel Proust on Art and Literature*, 298) and, mainly, how should one interpret his unchanged friendship, also in later years, with the extremely anti-Semitic and violent Léon, a co-sponsor, with Charles Maurras, of the royalist and anti-Semitic newspaper *L'Action Française*, and active supporter of the Camelots du Roi, the youth squads of Maurras's movement, essentially a group of anti-Semitic rowdies? Had Proust deeply resented Daudet's views and political activity, he could not have dedicated to him the third volume of the novel, *The Guermantes Way*, published in 1921, as he did, and he couldn't have kept friendly relations with him, notwithstanding his intimacy with Léon's brother Lucien, but he did. There is more: sometime in 1921 or early 1922, Proust wrote an article on Léon Daudet's *Souvenirs* that he himself defined as "dithyrambic" (the article was probably never published, but the unfinished text was eventually printed posthumously). Proust declared in it that he did not share Daudet's political views, but in *Souvenirs*, he stated, it is "the poet, and only the poet who speaks"; Proust, in his praise knew no bounds (*Marcel Proust on Art and Literature*, 396–98 and 416).

I may be speaking from a post–Second World War viewpoint, but one cannot escape some facts: Proust couldn't help admiring one of the chief French anti-Jewish agitators of his day. Clearly, his feelings toward Jews and his own Jewishness were utterly confused at best, notwithstanding his attitude against injustice in the Dreyfus Affair; and all of this, notwithstanding being aware of his own Jewish heritage. Or was it because of it?

The identity issue in the novel extends well beyond the Narrator's specific dilemmas regarding Jewishness. In general terms, three identity categories appear in the Narrator's description of characters: the glorious, the self-evident, the shameful.

There is no need, I suppose, to spend much time in identifying the hierarchy of those identities I qualified as glorious, a hierarchy essentially accepted by its own group, the aristocracy. The Narrator describes at great length the politics of aggrandizement of various families belonging to that exalted class, but none of them would, for example, have questioned that the Guermantes were at the top of the pyramid. There couldn't be much dispute about rankings carved by history into the minds of all the caste's members. This or that member may have been shunned because of specific circumstances, but ultimately, all shared the pride of lineages that in their minds distinguished them from common mortals.

The identity of the native French bourgeoisie and of French people in general, as they appear in the novel, is not debated in any way, as it is self-evident. But it is within this category that the Narrator identifies a kind of hidden aristocracy, represented by his servant Françoise, her habits, and at times mysterious code of behavior, which "nothing in [her] background or in her career as a servant in a village household could have put into her head; and," the Narrator goes on, "we were obliged to assume that there was latent in her some past existence in the ancient history of France, noble and little understood, as in those manufacturing towns where old mansions still testify to their former courtly days" (*Search*, I, 37–38). What applies to Françoise applies no less to the other inhabitants of Combray, apparently similar to the servant's own hometown, and where she lived and worked for the Narrator's Aunt Léonie, totally immersed in and belonging to that rural environment. And let's remember, it s the Combray ancestry, that of *la France profonde* ("deep France"), that the Narrator attributes to his mother. In other words, the Narrator's mother doesn't partake in any way in the third category of identities: the shameful one, although the Narrator is never sure of what he believes regarding that crucial issue.

Shameful identity is not uncommon in the novel. First and foremost, notwithstanding our doubts about his own choice, the Narrator exercises his sarcasm about those Jews intent on discarding their unfortunate heritage: Swann's daughter, Gilberte, who gleefully adopts the name de Forcheville; Bloch, who becomes Jacques du Rozier; and, indirectly, the Narrator's mother, whose change of identity I just mentioned, as well, of course, as the Narrator himself. It also applies, on a different register, to the hidden inverts, so numerous in the novel, who are secret pariahs like the new-fangled ex-Jews; the inverts' fate, as we saw, the Narrator likens to that of the Jews. But there are more: the violinist Morel, who desperately hides his origins as a servant's son; Legrandin, the perfect snob, who suffers from not belonging to the aristocracy, and possibly Albertine, the orphaned girl, adopted by relatives.

And yet... after she marries Saint-Loup and becomes a member of the aristocracy, Gilberte mentions her Jewish father again; Swann himself, in the last years of his life and probably because of the Dreyfus Affair, becomes more conscious of his Jewishness and, according to the Narrator, closer to his ancestry. Whatever one may think of that sort of "conversion," the Narrator explains, as mentioned above, that Jews are persecuted pariahs, like homosexuals, which explains and probably justifies hiding one's identity. In other words, at this point of our analysis, one cannot be sure what the author/Narrator's position may have been regarding the acceptance or the discarding of one's Jewish identity. He may have agreed with either one of such personal decisions. Did he deeply care about the issue? At the private level probably not; at the public level, probably yes, as with his second thoughts about too much praise for homosexuality.

Let's, for the time being, leave identity problems aside and turn back to the novel's wider moral uncertainties. We encounter, among the interpreters of *In Search*, conclusions very different from those of Benjamin Taylor or Edmund Wilson: assessments that marginalize or don't mention the grandmother at all. Indeed, she appears only in the first third of the immense canvas and is rarely a point of reference later on, except for a short surge of grief long after her death. Thus, in his introduction to the twice-revised translation of the novel into English, the one used here, Richard Howard asks why Proust, like Tolstoy, a novelist writing between two centuries, is considered modern while Tolstoy is seen as traditional, as belonging to the nineteenth century. Howard's answer, which leads to the core of our problem, states convincingly that while traditional novelists still take such values as love, friendship, and loyalty at face value, Proust "declares [them] to be failures, in fact disasters" (*Search*, I, xvii–xviii).

Indeed, there is no love in the *Search* without betrayal and jealousy; there is no friendship that lasts over time, no loyalty except that imposed by social imperatives. But isn't that mostly the case within any society? It wouldn't be worth dwelling on if the novel didn't insist on a somewhat unusual category of betrayals: that of parents by their children and particularly of doting fathers by their daughters, as was the case with Gilberte, as we saw, and appears to be even more blatantly cruel in the case of Vinteuil's daughter.

In the Vinteuil episode, the Narrator, still almost a child, is vacationing as usual in Combray. Left alone for a day, he ventures to nearby Montjouvain, where the recently deceased composer Vinteuil lived with a daughter whom he cherished and who went on staying in her father's house after his death. The Narrator falls asleep, and when he wakes up he finds himself in full view of the Vinteuil living room, illuminated and with open shutters. He thus becomes the involuntary observer of a slow-motion lesbian ritual taking place between Vinteuil's daughter and her lover, who arrived in the meantime. The ritual reaches its psychological climax as both girls are about to spit on a photograph of the composer the daughter had set out, a performance the Narrator can't see anymore, as the shutters have been closed.

The unexpected sequel to this scene is the complicated and tortuous interpretation that the Narrator then offers of the true nature of Vinteuil's daughter: she is good and sensitive in essence and takes part in this desecration under some kind of false pretense:

> It was not evil that gave her the idea of pleasure, that seemed to her attractive; it was pleasure, rather, that seemed evil. And as, each time she indulged in it, it was accompanied by evil thoughts such as ordinarily had no place in her virtuous mind, she came at length to see in pleasure itself something diabolical, to identify it with Evil. Perhaps Mlle Vinteuil felt that at heart her friend was not altogether bad, not really sincere when she gave vent to these blasphemous utterances. At any rate, she had the pleasure of receiving and returning those kisses, those smiles, those glances, all feigned, perhaps, but akin in their base

and vicious mode of expression to those which would
have been evinced not by an ordinary kind, suffering person but by a cruel and wanton one. She could
delude herself for a moment that she was indeed en-
joying the pleasures which, with so perverted an ac-
complice, a girl might enjoy who really did harbour
such barbarous feelings towards her father's memory.
Perhaps she would not have thought of evil as a state
so rare, so abnormal, so exotic, one in which it was
so refreshing to sojourn, had she been able to discern
in herself, as in everyone else, that indifference to the
sufferings one causes which, whatever other names
one gives it, is the most terrible and lasting form of
cruelty. (*Search*, I, 232–33)

Tortuous indeed. Of course, one cannot out-Proust
Proust, but one may try... The desecration performed together by the two lovers has often been discussed as alluding to the author's sadistic rites of profanation aimed at his
beloved mother's memory. I mentioned that I would return
to this issue: the author, according to some testimonies,
brought the mother's furniture and photos to a brothel for
homosexuals that he indeed patronized and had some of the
"staff" spit on the photos, etc.

Strangely enough, the Narrator mentions giving some of
the furniture that had belonged to Aunt Léonie to a regular brothel he had visited a few times: "I ceased moreover
to go to this house because, anxious to present a token of

my good-will to the woman who kept it and was in need of furniture, I had given her a few pieces—notably a big sofa—which I had inherited from my aunt Léonie... But as soon as I saw them again in the house where these women were putting them to their own uses, all the virtues that pervaded my aunt's room at Combray at once appeared to me, tortured by the cruel contact to which I had abandoned them in their defencelessness! Had I outraged the dead, I would not have suffered such remorse" (*Search*, II, 208). Should this apparent confession be taken seriously or were these few fictional lines the source of the rumors?

The rumors were fed by an external source and by a few other lines from Proust's writings. Externally they were peddled by a totally unreliable and unsavory character, Maurice Sachs, a homosexual writer and a notorious scandalmonger. Sachs knew Proust and Proust knew Sachs and his reputation, which makes it highly unlikely that he would have confided such intimate—and indeed quite scandalous—details of his life to a man like him.

Julia Kristeva's argument from *Proust and the Sense of Time*, which I referenced as interpreting the Vinteuil incident as a profanation of the mother, was strongly influenced by Georges Bataille's essay "Marcel Proust et la mère profanée," and is based on Sachs but also on some further texts. "Over the years 1908 to 1912, the Proustian idea of profaning the mother takes root," Kristeva writes. "Notebook 1 [one of those Proust used for drafts] refers to 'the mother's face in a debauched grandson.' Profanation is seen as a condition of sublimation. In *Against Sainte-Beuve* [a text of 1909, parts of which will belong to *In Search*] we read: 'The face of a son who lives on, like a monstrance in which a sublime mother, now dead, placed all her faith, is like the profanation of a sacred memory.' In *Sodom and Gomorrah*, finally, there is this late addition to the text: 'Moreover was it possible to separate M. de Charlus's appearance completely from the fact that, as sons do not always bear a likeness to their fathers, even when they are not inverts and go after women, they consummate in their faces the profanation of their mothers? But let us leave at this point what would be worth a chapter on its own: 'profanation of the mother'" (Kristeva, *Proust and the Sense of Time*, 20). The quotes seem to be telling, but as their context has little to do with the Vinteuil episode, we are back at the rumors as the source of interpretation.

What could add some verisimilitude to the rumors about profanation of the mother resides possibly in the Narrator's efforts (in a sequence much longer than my quote) to prove the Vinteuil daughter's intrinsic goodness. One cannot avoid the impression that the Narrator is telling us "all of this is true and was irresistible but, at heart, the daughter remains a loving daughter notwithstanding her shameful playacting."

The same intention is apparent in the second major episode of sadomasochism (in fact, straightforward masochism). It is linked again to sexual inversion, and appears close to the end of the novel, in Paris during the war. The Narrator strolls in streets darkened by curfew. Driven by thirst, he notices a building from which shines a feeble light and decides to try his luck. As he approaches the gate, he sees a man coming out as silently and unobtrusively as possible. He recognizes him by his way of walking; it is his once-closest friend, now at the front: Robert de Saint-Loup. The Narrator enters, and to his amazement finds himself in the reception room of a brothel for homosexuals. The Narrator had already previously known of Saint-Loup's secret life, but here it was, as obvious as could be.

In the course of the Narrator's visit to the brothel, he manages to watch, unseen, the Baron de Charlus's flagellation. The flagellation scene is described as something of a comedy: Charlus wants brutal hoodlums to beat him, but gets—and knows it—only peaceful and ordinary men who attempt to impersonate the criminals he wishes for. In fact, throughout the novel Charlus, notwithstanding his gruff posturing, appears as a generous and highly educated member of the Guermantes clan. Here the Narrator convincingly shows the genuinely soft personality of a masochist. The similarity with the Vinteuil episode, as far as the personality of the "victim" is concerned, is blatant.

Another interpretation remains possible, which is that the identification of the desecrated character with the mother derives from the Narrator's account, as rumors about the author's rituals were probably spreading after the publication of *Swann's Way* and even more so after Proust's death. But, if one leaves aside these unprovable rumors and simply follows the Narrator's rendition, then, in the first case, we face the desecration of a father's image and, thereafter, that of a father figure, the kind that Charlus may have represented for the young "thugs." Moreover, in the first case, the furniture given to the brothel is Aunt Léonie's furniture, and Léonie was the father's sister. Thus, back we are at the profanation of the father. Whomever, father or mother, the target may have been, we discover deep resentment once again at the fringe of wanton cruelty.

In the *Search*, cruelty is all-pervasive and depicted from all possible angles. It appears from the early pages of the novel, when the Narrator's grandmother, during evenings in Combray, is compelled to witness helplessly how her husband, encouraged by the diners' jovial comments, enjoys the alcohol dangerous to his health. One finds this cruelty at every social level: it taints the behavior of Françoise (who, after Léonie's death will become the longtime servant of the Narrator's family) toward her pregnant kitchen help: "Françoise had adopted, to minister to her unfaltering resolution to render the house uninhabitable to any other servant, a series of stratagems so cunning and so pitiless that, many years later, we discovered that if we had been fed on asparagus day after day throughout that summer, it was because their smell gave the poor kitchen-maid who had to prepare them such violent attacks of asthma that she was finally obliged to leave my aunt's service" (*Search*, I, 173).

In fact, this was not Françoise's worst manifestation of cruelty—a cruelty that was somehow unintentional, as if it were part of her nature. As the Narrator's grandmother lay dying, the old servant was ready to sacrifice sleep and any rest to assist with constant care, but at the same time she took manifestly cruel initiatives. Thus she insisted on combing her moribund mistress's hair: "When I came into the room," the Narrator tells us, "I saw between the cruel hands of Françoise . . . beneath aged straggling tresses which scarcely had the strength to withstand the contact of the comb, a head which, incapable of maintaining the position into which it had been forced, was rolling about in a ceaseless whirl in which sheer debility alternated with spasms of pain." The Narrator intervenes just as Françoise is fetching a mirror to show her mistress, from whom all mirrors had been kept away, the beautiful work she had done (*Search*, III, 454).

Later, the maître d'hôtel's cruelty toward Françoise remains within the confines of jests, while that of the ultra-wealthy Verdurins toward the weakest member of their own group, the humble Saniette, and of the same Verdurins against the socially preeminent but emotionally weak Charlus reveals sheer sadism in the upper middle class. It permeates the daily dismissiveness and the ingrained feelings of incontrovertible superiority that members of every rank of the aristocratic pyramid express against those considered one peck lower. All of this is in no way specific to the universe described by the Narrator, except that this frequent stressing of cruelty may indicate a deeply pessimistic vision of the world. It does not call for compassion, but for irony, at times for sarcasm.

The paradoxical aspect of the cruelty attributed by the Narrator to the otherwise softhearted baron, immediately appears in the explanation: "In taking sides against the Germans [during the war] he would have seemed to himself to be acting as he did only in his hours of physical pleasure, to be acting, that is, in a manner contrary to his merciful nature, fired with passion for seductive evil and helping to crush virtuous ugliness" (*Search*, VI, 126). In short, the cruelty apparent in the baron's sexual games is merely an imaginary cruelty. In the pages that follow the scene at the brothel, the Narrator returns several times to the theme of the pseudo-cruelty of inverts. Why? It seems to me that here the Narrator is revealing what the author hid and yet confessed to André Gide (who would not have invented the facts): to achieve orgasm, Proust needed at times to watch the cruel scene of two starved rats, brought in a cage, tearing at each other (Carter, *Marcel Proust*, 610–611).

To bolster the case against true cruelty in the novel, the Narrator shows redeeming traits in each of the characters painted with the harshest brush, starting with his father. "In the case of my grandmother and mother it was only too clear that their severity towards me was deliberate on their part and indeed cost them dear, but perhaps even my father's coldness too was only an external aspect of his sensibility" (*Search*, V, 136). Although the expatiation that follows, meant to confirm the existence of this secret sensitivity—a dual personality characteristic inherited by the Narrator—is ultimately presented with a question mark, it proves nonetheless to be a general trait in the Narrator's psychological panorama.

The most despicable characters show their good side in due time: the lesbian friend of Vinteuil's daughter takes it upon herself to save the composer's work by uncovering and copying it; M. Verdurin, whose brutality toward Saniette is described on several occasions, decides to establish a fund to help the penniless Saniette after he is felled by a stroke; Gilberte, later in life, abandons the camouflage of her origins. In short, the moral duality of human nature as such appears as an axiom of the Narrator's view of the world. Even the despicable Morel, Charlus's and later Saint-Loup's lover, appears somehow redeemed by his absolute devotion to art and his rejection of any compromise that could touch this sacred domain.

The epitome of such duality is, of course, the Baron de Charlus. Under the pretense of virility hides a woman. Under the pretense of sadism hides a sensitive and generous being. And this man with "the appearance of a Great Inquisitor painted by El Greco" (*Search*, V, 272) speaks at times with a falsetto voice. It may be that the traditional representation of male homosexuality inspired the Narrator to turn human duality into a general law.

This psychological intuition makes the task of the future novelist, the future author of the novel that he, the Narrator, is about to start writing, particularly complex: "This writer—who, moreover, must bring out the opposed facets of each of his characters in order to show its volume—would have to prepare his book with meticulous care" (*Search*, VI, 507).

This being said, however, apart from the composite mother/grandmother, whose possessiveness is redeemed of course by her unquestioned love for the Narrator, a love that the Narrator reciprocates while also resenting aspects of it, there is no mutual love in the *Search* and no truly admirable personality; in other words, there is nothing comparable to the feelings that grow between Frédéric Moreau and Madame Arnoux in Flaubert's *Sentimental Education*, to the personality of a Pierre Bezukhov in Tolstoy's *War and Peace*, or to that of Alyosha in Dostoevsky's *The Brothers Karamazov*. On the other hand, any negative trait finds some positive redeeming aspect.

If my interpretation is correct, there is no place for Evil (with a capital E) in the *Search*. On that point, I am in disagreement with Antoine Compagnon, the well-known Proust scholar, whose insistence on the close link between Baudelaire and Proust and, mainly, on the camouflaged presence of Evil in the Narrator (*Proust entre deux siècles*, 153 and following, and 302), doesn't take into account the difference between Evil (Mal)—which Baudelaire made the essence of his work—and baseness and even everyday cruelty in Proust's novel, with the mitigating excuses I discussed above. But what there is plenty of in Proust's Narrator is irony.

The Narrator's irony is essentially literary and social. The author's literary irony has been honed for years by his parodying the style and form of writing of many a predecessor or contemporary author; it reappears in *Time Regained* (the title of the last volume) as the Narrator's highly amusing parody of Edmond de Goncourt. However, literary irony is of minor importance in the *Search* when compared to the ubiquity of social irony.

No group, no individual, escapes the Narrator's sometimes mild, mostly acerbic descriptions. The parochialism of Combray's inhabitants, including the local members of Mamma's family, is usually the object of good-natured humor: they exemplify the deep sleep, the closed mind of much of provincial France at the beginning of the twentieth century. In fact, the irony directed at the provincial mind, including a sample of local grandees from Brittany and Normandy whom the Narrator observes during his first stay at Balbec, is light compared to what is in store for the capital's wealthy bourgeoisie, represented by the Verdurins and their "salon" and of course for the cream of Paris aristocracy, the Faubourg Saint-Germain, the Guermantes and their entourage.

The Narrator doesn't describe the haute bourgeoisie, the Verdurins, as boorish. Madame Verdurin is aware of the latest artistic trends and creations and shows a highly educated taste, mainly in music, dance, and the theater. But not so fast: the lady is despotic, to say the least, and extraordinarily manipulative in the handling of her guests, the members of her salon, who either have to strut on her stage according to her whims or be excluded. During the war, she pretends to be in touch daily with the high command and thus spreads the most inane news every day. And as hundreds of thousands are killed, she will have no rest before managing to get her usual croissants again. Here she is at breakfast, as she reads about the sinking of the *Lusitania* and exclaims, "How horrible!... This is something more horrible than the most terrible stage tragedy." As the Narrator continues, "the death of all these drowned people must have been reduced a thousand million times before it impinged upon her, for even as, with her mouth full, she made these distressful observations, the expression which spread over her face, brought there...by the savour of that so precious remedy against headaches, the croissant, was in fact one of satisfaction and pleasure" (*Search*, VI, 120–21).

Madame Verdurin's regular guests are not on the same cultural level as the "Patronne" (except for Swann, who briefly attended her dinners, before the Narrator was born; thus the Narrator has merely heard of that earlier period). The guests, the Verdurins' "circle," are a few artists, a faded Russian aristocrat, and members of the professions, some with little culture and knowledge outside of their domain, such as the physician Cottard (whom we already met), others with immense erudition, like the Sorbonne professor Brichot, but with a ridiculous and at times insufferable need to display it: they offer the Narrator a rich gallery of somewhat foolish characters on whom heaping ridicule is a must.

The Faubourg is dealt with even more sarcastically. At its highest reaches, an appearance of culture and refinement hides ignorance and poor taste. Moreover, egotism, backbiting, and total indifference to the feelings of others are all-pervasive. As we saw earlier, when Swann, a "close and cherished friend" of Oriane de Guermantes and of her husband, the Duc de Guermantes, tries to tell the duchess that he is terminally ill, she hears but waves him off, as she is getting late for a dinner and, moreover, has to change shoes . . . and Oriane is the most refined, the most cultivated, the most intelligent of the tribe: she is the summit.

On the face of it, the Narrator's generalized irony appears as the genuine expression of his feelings and seems to offer the most decisive proof of the need to separate the Narrator from the author. After all, Proust's close friends belonged either to the haute bourgeoisie (his own family, the Straus couple, and many others) or to the aristocracy (Bertrand de Fénelon, Montesquiou of course, the Princess Soutzo, and many others again), and these links didn't change to the very end. Had the issue been raised—not that it ever was, as far as we know—the author could have argued that the Narrator was autonomous from him. And the Narrator's critical gaze cannot be put in doubt. Yet, as in the case of the individual characters, each class has its saving grace in the novel: Mme Verdurin's taste and culture, her pro-Dreyfus position, her social acumen; the Faubourg's refinement and, at the level of Prince and Princesse de Guermantes, the secret pro-Dreyfus change of mind. Thus, mainly regarding the aristocracy, what transpires behind the acerbic description? Could it be, that notwithstanding what he observes, the Narrator cannot help admiring those who dwell quite naturally at such exalted heights and doesn't he feel genuine pride at being accepted by them? But doesn't he fool himself about the degree of their acceptance?

In fact, Proust must have sensed that he would never be truly accepted by the aristocracy, first for not being "born," and then for being a Jew; he had sufficient proof of his lowly rank in their feudal hierarchy, whether from the humiliating table placing on the occasion of banquets or from not being invited to more restricted events. Thus, as a recent study rightly argues, regarding the world of the Duchesse de Guermantes (a composite portrait of Geneviève Straus, Laure de Chevigné, and Élisabeth Greffulhe), the author's admiration and the Narrator's sarcasm ultimately belong to one and the same person (Weber, *Proust's Duchess*, 16 and following).

It reminds one of Hannah Arendt's distinction in *The Origins of Totalitarianism* between Jews as "pariahs" and Jews as "parvenus," which was common precisely during that turn of the century when the *Search* was born. For several years, Alfred Dreyfus was the epitome of the pariah. And one could say that Marcel, even after becoming the Narrator, was something of a parvenu, as seen from the Faubourg Saint-Germain.

I n Proust there is little dying altogether," Taylor noted, comparing *In Search* to George Eliot's *Middlemarch*, Tolstoy's *War and Peace*, and Thomas Mann's *Buddenbrooks*. He added:

"Having dramatized the death of the grandmother in *The Guermantes Way*, he'll dramatize that of Bergotte in *The Captive* and will then have had enough of dying" (Taylor, *Proust*, 85–86). The remark is not convincing to me. The Narrator may well not describe death on more than the two occasions mentioned by Taylor, but he discusses death in general and his own death at length in several episodes.

It is true that, notwithstanding some deeply felt reflections, the theme is kept within narrow limits, possibly untypical in modern European literature; it may lead us to a general remark about an emotional characteristic of Proust's chef d'oeuvre: it is a social satire on the grandest scale and an incomparable analysis of complex emotional constructs, but it mostly lacks a sense of tragedy. And here we accede to the wider aspects of this "moral accounting."

At some point, in his conversations with Albertine, a chance remark leads the Narrator to a discussion of modern writers, particularly Stendhal, Thomas Hardy, and Fyodor Dostoevsky. This, of course, is but a short conversation on a topic of which Proust was a master, but that Albertine could not have sustained. (For more on Proust's vast and deep knowledge of classical and modern literature, see his *Contre Sainte-Beuve* and, among many specialized studies, Anka Muhlstein's *Monsieur Proust's Library* and Antoine Compagnon, *Proust entre deux siècles*.)

The main criticism, in the conversation with Albertine, that the Narrator directs to each of the authors aims at proving that from one novel to the next, quasi-identical patterns are used by each of them as symbolic markers and, more concretely, in the description of the main characters. "Isn't the Dostoievsky woman...with her mysterious face, whose engaging beauty changes abruptly, as though her apparent good nature was only play-acting, into terrible insolence (although at heart it seems that she is more good than bad), isn't she always the same...?" (*Search*, V, 508).

The Narrator's remarks may be applicable to some of Dostoevsky's women, but they do not fit his male characters. Gide devoted a convincing essay to the intrinsic difference between each of the brothers Karamazov (Gide's essay was published in 1923 but he lectured about it in 1922; Proust could have heard of the argument). In Gide's essay, while Ivan embodies cold intellect, and Dimitry the world of passion, it is Alyosha, the youngest brother, who represents the religious dimension, the intimation of transcendence.

Let me add that the Narrator's remark regarding Dostoevsky's female types is puzzling, as the Narrator himself writes, when reflecting on memory, that he aims at discovering general characteristics under the appearance of diversity: "There is a feeling for generality which, in the future writer, itself picks out what is general and can for that reason one day enter into a work of art" (*Search*, VI, 306).

Notwithstanding the Narrator's ability to discern under general traits the tiniest nuances in the emotional relations of his characters, the most ephemeral and also the most steadily recurring characteristics in their social behavior, there is no place in the whole *In Search* for any aspiration aiming beyond these limits, except for the cult of beauty in all its manifestations. There is nothing about the cult of beauty in Dostoevsky's novels, but there is nothing about some ultimate questions, about preoccupations with any kind of transcendence, in Proust. In other words, in Proust there is no place for sin and redemption as there is in Dostoevsky, or in Tolstoy for that matter. The author was agnostic, but that should be irrelevant regarding the immense expanse of human types described. We miss the tragic dimension and we miss the metaphysical one or what could also be the affirmation of human freedom and self-assertion (or self-creation), such as is found less than two decades later in Existentialism. As Jacques Rivière, Proust's editor at Gallimard and a friend during the last years of his life, put it: "After the self-satisfied inwardness of Romanticism, Proust came along, determined not to give the least credence to the 'Sirènes intérieures.' Proust approaches experience without the slightest metaphysical interest... without the slightest tendency to console" (quoted in Walter Benjamin, "The Image of Proust," *Illuminations*, 213).

In the course of the same conversation with Albertine, the Narrator explains: "I'm not a novelist; it's possible that creative writers are tempted by certain forms of life of which they have no personal experience..." (*Search*, V, 510–11). Possibly the author of *In Search* should have been subjected to that kind of temptation. It could also be that by staying within the limits of his personal experience, Proust created a psychological and moral world of vast complexity, but within a very specific moral mold.

Clearly then, the only value that the Narrator considered an absolute was artistic/literary creation (the cult of beauty). Once he discovered that he possessed the creativity that would allow him to become a true writer, he understood that his years of idleness, those years he previously considered wasted, would now become the essential material for the construction of his novel.

The Narrator is never disappointed by Vinteuil's music or by Elstir's paintings; and, to my mind, some of the most beautiful pages written on Wagner's music in a novel can be found in the *Search* (see, for example, V, 205 and following). This being said, the writer whom he had admired for a long time, an older contemporary and something of a mentor whom he often met, the late Bergotte (a stand-in for Anatole France), also the only French novelist of his day whom he discussed on several occasions and at length, leaves him now completely unimpressed. The Narrator, back in Paris after a long absence, is in the Prince de Guermantes's library, leafing through a Bergotte novel, waiting for a musical performance to end so that he can be admitted to the drawing room and attend the princesse's matinee.

The Narrator, even if he is right, may not be entirely disinterested. He knows now that he can write and will write. Thus he wants to assure himself that, at least regarding French contemporary literature, no comparison can be possible between him and those writers who had, in the eyes of many, dominated the scene up to the most recent past. But then, if he dismisses Bergotte or any other contemporary French author, are there any literary creations he is dreaming about as models? There are two, both of them very far from contemporary France: Saint-Simon's *Memoirs* and *The Arabian Nights*.

.5.

THE ARABIAN NIGHTS

J ames Joyce once quipped about *Ulysses*: "I have put in so many enigmas and puzzles that it will keep the professors busy for centuries arguing about what I meant." If there is one author who can compete with the mischievous Irishman in that domain, it is Proust in the *Search*; the Narrator's very frequent references to *The Arabian Nights* may be one of these—nonetheless easily solved—puzzles.

The Arabian Nights (*Les contes de mille et une nuits*, or "The Tales of a Thousand and One Nights") is a collection of tales told every night to the Caliph of Bagdad by his wife Scheherazade, who leaves each story unfinished but concludes it on the next night before immediately starting another one that, again, will be left unfinished and so on, in order to whet the caliph's curiosity and thus postpone the execution that would befall her, as it did all previous one-night wives of the monarch, as a revenge for his first wife's infidelity. A few of those tales had become beloved children's stories (Ali Baba, Aladdin, Sinbad the Sailor) that were also read by the Narrator in Combray.

"My book," the Narrator writes, "though it might be as long as the *Arabian Nights*, would be entirely different"; thus the Narrator muses about his future creation. "True, when you are in love with some particular book, you would like yourself to write something that closely resembles it, but this love of the moment must be sacrificed, you must think not of your own taste but of a truth which far from asking you what your preferences are forbids you to pay attention to them. And only if you faithfully follow this truth will you sometimes find that you have stumbled again upon what you renounced, find that, by forgetting these works themselves, you have written the *Arabian Nights* or the *Memoirs* of Saint-Simon of another age" (*Search*, VI, 525).

The *Memoirs* of Saint-Simon, that extraordinary description of the court of Louis XIV and of the Regency, is a thoroughly apposite reference for a Narrator who is about to become the greatest literary painter—or can we say pathologist?—of pre-eminent social segments of late nineteenth and early twentieth century France. But *The Arabian Nights*? This allusion is even stranger if we take into account the Narrator's intention to follow the flashes of his (involuntary) memory, as we shall see, to mold his forthcoming novel.

The Arabian Nights comes up time and again in the *Search* and establishes one more connection between the Narrator's decision to start writing and the world of his childhood. The plates at Aunt Léonie's house in Combray were decorated with themes from *The Arabian Nights* and the aunt loved them. "She would put on her spectacles and spell out: 'Ali Baba and the Forty Thieves,' 'Aladdin and his Wonderful Lamp,' and smile, and say: 'Very good, very good'" (*Search*, I, 77). But how could this book be an indirect inspiration for the forthcoming novel that's close to an autobiography?

On the occasion of the trip she makes to Balbec with her son, the Narrator's mother gives him for his birthday two presents he'd asked for: the two French translations from the Arabic original (the one by Galland and the other by Mardrus) of *The Arabian Nights*. The Narrator alludes to the memory of Combray it evoked for him, but manifestly there is more. He then mentions his mother's attitude: "After casting her eye over the two translations, my mother would have preferred that I should stick to Galland's . . . Happening upon certain of the tales, she had been revolted by the immorality of the subject and the coarseness of the expression . . . [Invoking] on every occasion the opinion [her mother] would have expressed, my mother could have no doubt of the unfavourable judgment which my grandmother would have passed on Mardrus's version" (*Search*, IV, 318–19). She nonetheless gives both translations to her son, who incidentally must have been in his late teens at that time, according to the hazy computation allowed by the novel.

The coarse eroticism of many of the tales—certainly not those read in Combray—must have whetted the Narrator's interest, as it whetted the caliph's curiosity. It may also have been a potential inspiration for scenes that were to be inserted in his future work. This isn't an unwarranted hypothesis. Let's first remember the obvious significance of *François le champi* and of Madame de Sévigné's *Letters*. The symbolism of *The Arabian Nights* isn't more mysterious. The book is brought up twice as the narrator is leaving Jupien's brothel for homosexuals, after having witnessed Charlus's flagellation scene. The house, he tells Jupien, "is a veritable pandemonium. I thought that I had arrived, like the caliph in the *Arabian Nights*, in the nick of time to rescue a man who was being beaten, and in fact it was a different tale from the *Arabian Nights* which I saw enacted before me, the one in which a woman who has been turned into a dog willingly submits to being beaten in order to recover her former shape."

Jupien's answer is rather astonishing, if we recall that the former tailor has since become the manager of a brothel, a pander, and, occasionally, Charlus's valet, in other words somebody who usually doesn't dabble in literature. Be that as it may, he answers the Narrator in this way: "'You have mentioned one or two of the tales in the *Arabian Nights*,' he said. 'But there is another I know of, not unrelated to the title of a book which I think I have seen at the Baron's' (he was alluding to a translation of Ruskin's *Sesame and Lilies* which I had sent M. de Charlus). 'If ever you are curious, one evening, to see, I will not say forty but a dozen thieves, you have only to come here; to know whether I am in the house you have only to look up at that window; if I leave my little window open with a light visible it means that I am in the house and you may come in; it is my private Sesame. I say only Sesame. As for Lilies, if they are what you seek I advise you to go elsewhere'" (*Search*, VI, 206–7).

Jupien's retort contains two very different allusions. The first evokes Ruskin's book, which the author had indeed translated himself. As the Narrator never wrote a single word about the books the author had written or translated, in order, no doubt, to leave intact the function of involuntary memory as the trigger of literary creation—a theme I will address at length—this allusion is a discreet mention that, notwithstanding this centrality of memory, the author / Narrator had produced much literary work in the years preceding the coming illumination.

The second allusion hints at the real establishment that was known to the author. Proust visited Le Cuziat's brothel and employed young prostitutes for masturbation sessions (Carter, *Marcel Proust*, 609–12). In other words, the Narrator couldn't avoid such an essential theme and, instead of transposing it into a brothel with female prostitutes, he kept a truthful allusion to what was otherwise well hidden in the novel. Thus we see once more that the function of the Narrator who is the author but isn't is to hide aspects of the author's life but also, sometimes in the same few lines, to hint at them in a sufficiently camouflaged way.

Saint-Simon's *Memoirs* and *The Arabian Nights* point to two major themes of *In Search*. The first indicates the stupendous social satire that the reader encounters, while *The*

Arabian Nights announce the many facets of love relations dissected within the novel: the same-sex relations the Narrator was surrounded with, as well as the different facets of all love relations, the desire that fires them, the jealousy they entail, and the immense grief they can provoke.

The Narrator hints at the resemblance of the author's fate with that of Scheherazade. Both used stories, told at night, night after night, to escape death (once he started writing *In Search*, Proust worked on the novel at night and slept during the day). When the Narrator, facing old age, wonders whether he still has enough time to accomplish what has now become his sole aim in life before the inexorable end, he decides that night after night he will tell his tales and try to outsmart death: "By day, the most I could hope for was to try to sleep. If I worked, it would be only at night. But I should need many nights, a hundred perhaps, or even a thousand. And I should live in the anxiety of not knowing whether the master of my destiny might not prove less indulgent than Sultan Shahriyar, whether in the morning, when I broke off my story, he would consent to a further reprieve and permit me to resume my narrative the following evening. Not that I had the slightest pretension to be writing a new version, in any way, of the *Arabian Nights*, or of that other book written by night, Saint-Simon's *Memoirs*" (*Search*, VI, 524).

The many facets of love in *The Arabian Nights*? Indeed, except for one: reciprocal heterosexual love. The Narrator

doesn't recognize anything of the kind. Consider his avoidance, in his discussions of literature with Albertine (about
Stendhal, Thomas Hardy, or Dostoevsky) of any serious
mention of Flaubert, an author that Proust knew inside out
and greatly admired. Thus, the Narrator's avoidance may
have been intentional. In the novel, reference to the author
of *Sentimental Education* is limited to silly remarks from two
of the characters and to an entirely inconsequential aside by
the Narrator. That's all. And yet, if any other French novels could be compared to *In Search*, they belong to Balzac,
Stendhal, and Flaubert, in particular to his *Education* (Proust
wrote an essay about Flaubert's style before the war; it was
ultimately published in January 1920 in Gallimard's *Nouvelle
Revue Française*, aka the *NRF*).

I already mentioned, regarding *Education*, the love between Frédéric Moreau, the young provincial character,
intent on making it in Paris, and Madame Arnoux, a somewhat older and married woman; it was a sporadic love relation and one that was never sexually fulfilled. Does it mean
that had it been fulfilled it would necessarily have resulted
in disappointment and jealousy, like the love relations of *In
Search*? It is not the impression the reader receives, although
Flaubert doesn't offer any answer. But one could assume that
such a possibility ultimately led to Frédéric's disenchant-
ment, as expressed in his final conversation with his friend
Deslaurier.

Nonetheless, the major difference between both novels derives from the fact that in the *Education* the evolution

of a reciprocal love relationship is at center stage, while *In Search* doesn't admit the possibility of such mutual feelings. Of course, unilateral love has a long pedigree in French literature; one may also attribute the absence of reciprocity to the difference of historical context between Flaubert's and Proust's novels, although the relation between Swann and Odette belongs to the eighteen-seventies, in other words to a society which is not quintessentially different from that of the *Education*, which was published in 1869 and described events taking place during the July Monarchy, the Revolution of 1848, and the Second Empire.

One may also argue that in Combray, the Narrator experienced his love for his mother as "anguished" and that he saw it as occasionally nonreciprocal when Mamma couldn't come to kiss him good night, thus possibly determining his view of love throughout his adult life. All these hypotheses and more can and have been offered to explain the Narrator's description of love (Finch, "Love, sexuality and friendship," 168 and following) with the exception of the simplest, possibly because it looked so simple. It may be that *In Search* expresses the author's own disappointments, particularly regarding unrequited love for his driver-secretary, Alfred Agostinelli, and some previous unsuccessful homosexual attachments, as with the author's love for the diplomat Bertrand de Fénelon. They may have mattered more than any "anguished" childhood experience or the advent of modern literary cynicism.

.6.

THE NARRATOR

I t is time to turn to the author's central literary device, the one already briefly discussed in the introduction and on which I have based the main aspects of this essay: the figure and function of the Narrator. There have been many attempts to define the "Me" used by the Narrator. As the linguist Leo Spitzer put it, "this Me seems to be situated at greater depth [than the narrating Me and the acting Me]; he has left the surface of the story in an inaccessible deep level" (Spitzer, "Le style de Marcel Proust," *Études de style*, 451, my translation. I thank Carlo Ginzburg for drawing my attention to the importance of this essay).

Another more recent attempt at definition, with which I partly disagree, will be of indirect help: Brian Rogers's essay on "Proust's Narrator" in *The Cambridge Companion to Marcel Proust*.

"The Narrator is not Marcel Proust," Rogers writes. "He often borrows the eyes and the ears of the author and seems to possess the same encyclopaedic culture. But he is only a character in a story and his story contains only one event, the decision to write a book... The reader must take on trust what the Narrator chooses to tell us about himself. He has no name, we have no clear idea what he looks like. For long stretches of his book he disappears from view, leaving the reader to eavesdrop on conversations of people who seem oblivious of this man's existence. He is passive and transparent, everywhere and nowhere, sometimes a spy, often a voyeur turning up in unlikely situations, a disembodied presence unlike that in any novel before. But the mirror he offers the reader is so fascinating that we not only enter the world reflected in it, we inhabit the Narrator's body, see everything through his eyes and share his sensibility" (Rogers, "Proust's Narrator," 98).

If the Narrator was just expressing what one knows of the author's views, emotions, and attitudes, Rogers would be right. But the Narrator has a mind of his own, so to speak, and often conveys views one doesn't expect, views that may have escaped the author's mind and heart. Thus at times he looks like Proust's unconscious, independent from the author's conscious ego—and there I agree with Spitzer's attribution of great depth to the Narrator's "Me"—that suffices to give him a personality of his own. He has become a character among the characters of the novel. Even when he doesn't escape the author's surveillance, he doesn't look like the author's mere shadow.

From the very first lines of the novel we see the child struggling with sleep or disoriented for a moment when waking up, we see him listening to his great-aunt as she shows him Golo's sinister figure and Geneviève de Brabant's castle on the magic lantern, while she tells him the story; we see and feel his distress when his mother cannot come up to his room to kiss him good night, and so on. We follow the stages of the Narrator's life: we are informed about his feelings, about the books he reads, the walks he takes, the conversations he has; we encounter his first loves, we are told of his earliest sexual experiences, in short we follow the growth and evolution of a very specific character whom we tend to identify with the author, although we know that it isn't always he. And we know exactly the physical sensations that trigger the Narrator's sudden recognition that he can become the writer he dreamt of being and despaired of ever becoming. In the figure of the Narrator, any reader familiar with Proust's life will easily recognize what belongs to that life and when something else is at work.

The Narrator hasn't been created only to offer a mirror in which several hundred characters are reflected. At times he does hold that mirror, but as I have stressed, he also takes on an autonomous role and often expresses himself in encrypted messages. Moreover, he stumbles at times into revelations or pseudo-revelations that certainly tell more about the author than the author may have wanted his readers to know. In other words, the Narrator performs multiple functions, some of which we cannot foresee. In this unintentional role, he is like the golem who, in a famous Jewish legend, has escaped from the rabbi who created him and starts destroying the defenses the rabbi had erected against himself and against the enemy.

Proust may not have welcomed the metaphoric rabbi, and he probably would have considered the golem only a helpful instrument. He tried to write an autobiographical novel, *Jean Santeuil*, but didn't complete it. Doing so may, among other difficulties, have limited the material he could use in the future. Thus, if he wanted to be free to rework most of the huge amount of his stored observations, he had no other choice but to invent a fictional Narrator as his alter ego. But in a fiction driven by personal memory, and at times by involuntary memory, the inherent dynamic of such narration could and did lead beyond the limits set by the author. More often, of course, the author could send, quite intentionally, what I called "encrypted messages" in order to convey what he wished to convey to a select readership. And at other times he pressed the wrong button and a flow of revelations came tumbling down.

Fundamentally, when the author holds the reins, the Narrator fulfills a dual main function: he is the dreamy conveyor of an emotional world, that of childhood, of loves and of pain; he is also the sharp observer of the social currents that swirl around him. As a dreamer, he can unveil aspects and puzzles of the unconscious; as an observer, he is allowed to ferret out the most ridiculous features of the puppets strutting on the social stage, and also their darkest secrets.

This dual persona allows him to move from one world to the other and hold the whole story together.

It is around the sexual domain in general that the Narrator's allusions or equivocations are the most significant ways of revealing what he otherwise denies, as I indicated already in the chapter on forbidden love. Here I shall merely look again at the Narrator's chance visit to Jupien's homosexual brothel. The visit, triggered by the flimsiest of narrative inventions, thirst, is a barely hidden allusion to Proust's apparently regular attendance at Le Cuizat's quite similar institution. The detailed description of the goings-on inside the brothel proves to the most naive reader that the Narrator is well acquainted with that exclusive drawing room. As for the repeated worry of all those concerned, clients, staff, and manager, about absolute discretion and the camouflage of clients' identity, isn't it an oblique reference to the author's similar worry, mainly after having been caught at least once in police raids?

No less significant is the allusion to Charlus's nickname among the staff, "the man in chains"; it is not too far away from Proust's nickname at Le Cuizat's place: "the rat man." (No allusion here to Freud's famous case, but rather, as already mentioned, to the habit the author confessed to André Gide, if orgasm could not be otherwise achieved.) Finally— and this may be the most significant allusion—in his mulling over the relations between Charlus and Morel, and after having assumed that Morel may have withheld all physical pleasure from the hungry baron, the Narrator comes to the conclusion that in any nonreciprocal love relationship, the partner who refuses to grant the sexual demands of the other holds the psychological advantage and can actually enjoy all the benefits of a generosity that will be more rewarding than it would have been in a fully reciprocal situation (*Search*, VI, 186–87). The Narrator isn't merely referring to the baron's love for Morel; he is very precisely describing Proust's unrequited passion for his driver and later secretary, Alfred Agostinelli.

And incidentally, don't the Narrator's allusions add some interesting details to the autobiographical dimension of the novel?

A nother function of the Narrator is, it seems to me, to be a sort of hyphen between the main characters and their distant past, thus giving to the immense story a further coherence and some of the harmony necessary to keep control over its expanse and its many facets. At times the Narrator points to the essential role played by a character in his own evolution, in the very genesis of the novel to be. Such is, for example, the role he attributes to Swann: "It occurred to me, as I thought about it, that the raw material of my experience, which would also be the raw material of my book, came to me from Swann, not merely because so much of it concerned Swann himself and Gilberte, but because it was Swann who from the days of Combray had inspired in me the wish to go to Balbec...and but for this I should never have known Albertine...Swann had been of primary importance, for had I not gone to Balbec I should never have known the Guermantes either, since my grandmother would not have renewed her friendship with Mme de Villeparisis nor should I have made the acquaintance of Saint-Loup and M. de Charlus and thus got to know the Duchesse de Guermantes and through her her cousin, so that even my presence at this very moment in the house of the Prince de Guermantes, where out of the blue the idea of my work had just come to me (and this meant that I owed to Swann not only the material but also the decision), came to me from Swann" (*Search*, VI, 328–29).

In other words, the Narrator, thanks to his ubiquity, allows the author to present various facets of Swann and any other of his characters as seen by diverse protagonists and over any length of time. As Vladimir Nabokov puts it, "one essential difference exists between the Proustian and the Joycean methods of approaching their characters. Joyce takes a complete and absolute character, God-known, Joyce-known, then breaks it up into fragments and scatters these fragments over the space-time of his book. The good rereader gathers these puzzle pieces and gradually puts them together. On the other hand, Proust contends that a character, a personality, is never known as an absolute but always as a comparative one. He does not chop it up but shows it as it exists through the notions about it of other characters. And he hopes, after having given a series of these prisms and shadows, to combine them into an artistic reality" (Nabokov, "Lectures on Literature," 217).

This effusive attribution to Swann of paternity for the novel confirms, to a point, the Narrator's dual vision of Jews: on the one hand, the "shtetl," the Jewish crowd, the *petits juifs* (Bloch), on the other hand, the "grands Israélites" (Swann), a sarcastic distinction we owe, much later, to the novelist François Mauriac, but one that reflected, even after World War II—and certainly before and during the war— the self-perception of most French "Israelites." It was an obvious self-perception during the earlier decades of the twentieth century, certainly as seen from the vantage point of the author and the Narrator.

Yet whatever the social context of the Narrator's perception of different strata of the Jewish community may have been, he seems benevolent at times regarding the Jews as a distinct and persecuted entity. Thus, as he observes a weary Swann, stricken by terminal cancer, at the reception in the Prince de Guermantes's palatial home, his thoughts turn to Jewish fate: "Swann belonged to that stout Jewish race, in whose vital energy, its resistance to death, its individual members seem to share. Stricken severally by their own diseases, as it is stricken itself by persecution, they continue indefinitely to struggle against terrible agonies which may be prolonged beyond every apparently possible limit, when already one can see only a prophet's beard surmounted by a huge nose which dilates to inhale its last breath, before the hour strikes for the ritual prayers and the punctual procession of distant relatives begins, advancing with mechanical movements as upon an Assyrian frieze" (*Search*, IV, 141–42).

At times, the Narrator functions as an "enabler" of encounters that shed some additional light on characters we thought we knew well but who suddenly appear somewhat different than what we imagined. Take, for example, the conversation between Charlus and Brichot as they are about to leave a dinner at the Verdurins'; the baron tells us about aspects of Swann's personality that we didn't know. And this conversation as such is facilitated by a previously ongoing discussion between the Narrator and Charlus that Brichot joins. We knew that Swann was intensely jealous of the "attention" other men granted to Odette in the early period of their relationship, but we didn't know that he fought a duel with one of those admirers on one occasion (as the author once did, albeit for a different reason) or that he took Odette's sister as his mistress to convey his fury as a result of Odette's infidelities (*Search*, V, 402).

Mostly, however, the Narrator listens and reports what he hears, an essential function in a novel based more on conversations than on anything else. But the Narrator's acrobatic listening, as at times he pays attention to several simultaneous discussions or monologues, is constantly interspersed with his own short answers and mainly with his silent observations on what is being said or done all around him. Thus, in the midst of a conversation with the terminally ill Swann at the Prince de Guermantes's reception, the Narrator follows his interlocutor's gaze suddenly fastening upon the beautiful Marquise of Surgis-le-Duc, as he rises to greet her: "as soon as Swann, on taking the Marquise's hand, had seen her bosom at close range and from above, he plunged an attentive, serious, absorbed, almost anxious gaze into the depths of her corsage, and his nostrils, drugged by her perfume, quivered like the wings of a butterfly about to alight upon a half-glimpsed flower. Abruptly he shook off the intoxication that had seized him, and Mme de Surgis herself, although embarrassed, stifled a deep sigh, so contagious can desire prove at times" (*Search*, IV, 145). And the conversation, briefly interrupted, goes on.

This short scene and its opening paragraphs perfectly ex-emplify the Narrator's role and his extraordinary agility in fulfilling it. As the Narrator is conversing with Swann, he cannot help hearing the Baron de Charlus talking to Mme de Surgis, which leads him (the Narrator) to give us a rapid summary of Surgis's past, of the origin of her name, of her move, twice over, from the height of society to its bottom and back, in between Charlus's continued flood of comments about a painting that had belonged to the Surgis family, his alluding to Vermeer as he recognizes Swann, whom Surgis then greets, which leads to the scene above and to the Narra-tor's remarks about the contagion of sexual desire, before he resumes the interrupted conversation with Swann.

The conversation that follows shows a different facet of the Narrator's role in the overall structure of the novel. As he resumes talking to Swann, the Narrator asks him about the truth in what is being hinted regarding Charlus's sexual preferences. Swann denies the evidence, which was well known to the Narrator, who had witnessed a love-making scene between Charlus and Jupien. In the following part of the conversation, Swann confides to the Narrator the Prince de Guermantes's and his wife's belief in Dreyfus's innocence. Nobody else knows of it. Thus, in regard to the private lives of the characters and their public personae, the Narrator ultimately is the one who knows both the false appearances and the facts about each of them. The Narrator is the depositor of all the falsehoods swirling around and, sooner or later, of the facts as far as they can be known. *In Search* is no *Rashomon*: the author remains within the boundaries of a realism that he otherwise denounces.

Although conversations are arguably the essential stuff *In Search* is made of, they are encased in a myriad of observations about the characters, of course, but also by a myriad of descriptions of the surrounding world, the beauty of which, as transmitted by the Narrator, is overwhelming. It is this sheer magnificence that endows the novel with an unusual power, holding the reader in its embrace throughout an immense journey. And it is the Narrator who conveys to us that iridescence of all things. But could it be that, here, too much beauty is the trouble?

In the preceding pages, I showed the Narrator's main "official" faces: as the conscious and agile presenter and commentator of an immense story on one hand, and on the other hand as the revealer of what could be called the author's un-conscious in ways that most probably escaped Proust's at-tention. Up until now this second function has repeatedly been shown in various well-defined episodes, either under the guise of the Narrator's strange and unexpected con-structs, or under that of his no-less-strange and unexpected omissions. I will suggest here that the voice of the author's unconscious can be identified in a comment of the Narrator that reveals the structure of the entire novel in a very spe-cific and concrete way. This is a tall order, I know, but it is a hypothesis worth examining.

It has been common for Proust biographers interested in psychology to point to the symbolic moment of the mother's good-night kiss, particularly when it is desperately longed for, an occurrence so poignantly described by the Narrator in the early pages of the novel, as the traumatic and defining event of his life. The pealing of the garden bell in Combray, announcing the dinner guest's departure and the parents coming up for the night, or the child's sobs when the mother is allowed to join him, remain present in the author/Nar-rator's innermost being throughout life. It is after many decades that the Narrator hears the pealing of that garden bell again, as he attends the final matinee at the Princesse de Guermantes's, after having just decided to start writing.

> This notion of Time embodied, of years past but not
> separated from us, it was now my intention to empha-
> sise as strongly as possible in my work. And at this very

moment, in the house of the Prince de Guermantes, as though to strengthen me in my resolve, the noise of my parents' footsteps as they accompanied M. Swann to the door and the peal—resilient, ferruginous, interminable, fresh and shrill—of the bell on the garden gate which informed me that at last he had gone and that Mamma would presently come upstairs, these sounds rang again in my ears, yes, unmistakably I heard these very sounds, situated though they were in a remote past. And as I cast my mind over all the events which were ranged in an unbroken series between the moment of my childhood when I had first heard its sound and the Guermantes party, I was terrified to think that it was indeed this same bell which rang within me and that nothing I could do would alter its jangling notes. On the contrary, having forgotten the exact manner in which they faded away and wanting to re-learn this, to hear them properly again, I was obliged to block my ears to the conversations which were proceeding between the masked figures all round me, for in order to get nearer to the sound of the bell and to hear it better it was into my own depths that I had to re-descend. And this could only be because its peal had always been there, inside me, and not this sound only but also, between that distant moment and the present one, unrolled in all its vast length, the whole of that past which I was not aware that I carried about within me (*Search*, VI, 529).

When the Narrator evokes the scene of the mother's good-night kiss for the first time, he uses a magnificent metaphor, as one may remember: "But of late I have been increasingly able to catch, if I listen attentively, the sounds of the sobs which I had the strength to control in my father's presence, and which broke out only when I found myself alone with Mamma. In reality their echo has never ceased; and it is only because life is now growing more and more quiet round about me that I hear them anew, like those convent bells which are so effectively drowned during the day by the noises of the street that one would suppose them to have stopped, until they ring out again through the silent evening air" (*Search*, I, 49).

Let us leave aside the eventual significance of the bell in both quotes and turn to what appears as the essential similarity between both: the noise of daily life that, in both cases, intervenes between the initial pain and ecstasy of the child's anxious love for his mother and the moment, when life becomes quieter, that allows the Narrator to hear again the pristine sounds of childhood days. Wasn't the noise of those many years that went by between the two moments generated by the unconscious choice of the Narrator himself, the choice of an all-consuming social life with its endless, torrential din of pointless conversations? And isn't the "logic" of the Narrator's unconscious obvious? The Narrator's choice of those many years of an apparently senseless social life was triggered by the need to defend himself against the memory and the otherwise overpowering anxiety exuded by the childhood sobs or the pealing of the garden bell, the echo of whose sound never ceased to resonate in the depth of his soul.

In other words, the invisible structure which underlies the entire novel and which links the childhood, the vast expanse of Time lost as unconscious defense against the anxiety of the unredeemed font of childhood happiness and the moment, tens of years later, when the Narrator, prodded by the revelations of involuntary memory, decides to start writing, that invisible structure emerges from the recapturing of the temporarily hidden sounds surrounding the moment of pure maternal love.

.7.

TIME AND DEATH

Time is the invisible presence hovering over the main novels of some of Proust's contemporaries: James Joyce's single day of Leopold Bloom's peregrinations through Dublin, the city and the netherworld; the seven years of Thomas Mann's Hans Castorp's stay in the Alpine sanatorium. There is a mystical quality to the conceptions of time in both these novels, and even more so in H. G. Wells's time traveler's vision of a threatening future. In comparison, Proust's Narrator's forty years or so are distinctly down-to-earth, but the sense of emptiness that oozes from them is ultimately no less disquieting than all the other representations.

In Search is a novel about time, but with a twist: it is directed toward the future, fueled by the Narrator's constant hope, albeit a waning one, that he may become a writer. When the Narrator recognizes, late in life, that he can indeed become a writer, it is through a series of sudden reminiscences about his own past. The novel, one could say, is directed toward the future in order to recapture the past. This statement isn't as eccentric as it looks at first glance. Although the Narrator's wish to become a writer was born when he wrote a few paragraphs about the dance of the steeples of Martinville that he observed while riding home to Combray with his parents in Dr. Percepied's carriage, I suggest that the deeper impulse came from his urge to keep the memory of the enchanted days of his childhood and that of an ever-unique maternal love, notwithstanding growing resentment.

To the childhood memories of Combray, one should add the locations most connected to the Narrator's first love for Gilberte Swann: the gardens of the Champs-Elysées, where the Narrator played with Gilberte and her friends, and later Odette Swann's sumptuous Paris apartment, which Gilberte and her mother regularly invited him to. One may also add the first visit to Balbec and the encounter with the group of girls, the companions of Albertine . . .

Thus, first and foremost, the past that the Narrator wishes to recapture is a past under the sign of love, a past that simultaneously and mainly somewhat later, finds new life, a true life, in the Narrator's great love, Albertine. Is this a past that closes upon itself, as the scenes of old age close the Narrator's story, or does this past carry a message of renewal, as intimated by the presence of Gilberte's daughter at the Princesse de Guermantes's matinee? "I saw Gilberte coming across the room towards me ... I was astonished to see at her side a girl of about sixteen, whose tall figure was a measure of the distance which I had been reluctant to see. Time, colourless and inapprehensible Time ... had materialised itself in this girl, moulding her into a masterpiece, while correspondingly on me, alas! it had merely done its work" (*Search*, VI, 506). Time as end and renewal? Or can we speak of an "eternal return"? On several occasions, the Narrator alludes to Nietzsche but doesn't mention the philosopher's vision of time.

"For a long time I would go to bed early." This first sentence of the novel is the equivalent of "Call me Ishmael" or of "All happy families ", and of a few other unforgettable first sentences in world literature with, however, a possibly unique additional feature: it includes the key word of the title, the key theme of the entire novel, and is echoed by the very last word, six volumes later, in the standard English translation: "Time." This much is always mentioned, with the usual addition that the end was written at the very same time as the beginning, which explains the elegant symmetry in words and in themes.

As striking as the beginning and the end of the entire text is the novel's first section of the initial chapter: there, the Narrator literally swirls in time, seamlessly moving from the earliest childhood memories to events that occurred some thirty-five or forty years thereafter, from evenings in Combray to evenings in Tansonville and, all through, to nights, restful or difficult, and to awakenings in the diverse places to which his travels were to lead him. This first section also encompasses the two major events that will determine the Narrator's life: the drama of the good-night kiss and the revelation of involuntary memory. Everything points to the future and to the past and, thus, to the constant flow of time.

We do not know at which point in time the Narrator is evoking the diverse moments of his life in that first sequence, but manifestly he is reminiscing about those distant evenings, nights, and awakenings, after having decided to write, after the revelations of involuntary memory. He remembers previous moments, once disjointed, that are now, as he writes, parts of the continuity in time created by involuntary memory. In other words, we the readers are told a story of disjointed moments by a Narrator who has recovered the sense of the temporal continuity of that same story. Sometimes this creates confusion. Thus, when the young Narrator travels to Balbec for the first time, he clearly remembers that it was Swann who had recommended to him, a few years beforehand, this seaside destination and its "Persian" church. And years later this occurs again, but before the revelations of involuntary memory, the Narrator remembers the chain of momentous events that were born from Swann's initial recommendation. Aren't we facing temporal continuity before that continuity was established?

The Narrator's handling of time remains in fact something of a mystery throughout: The dates of events are hard to identify (when they are not mistaken); the narration of the phases and events of a life thus recovered seems often haphazard, with discontinuity between occurrences that should follow each other.

To my mind, the most striking example of that haphazardness is that of one of the key episodes of the narrator's life, the story of the cup of tea and of the miraculous memory of Combray that arose from it. At what moment of the Narrator's life did it occur? The mother, who prepared the tea, was present. If so, the decisive epiphany, the one that, according to the Narrator, opened the gates of memory and allowed him to begin writing, the revelation triggered by the uneven stones in the Guermantes's courtyard, happened much later. Does it mean that the Narrator kept the suddenly recovered memory of Combray without writing it down? The taste of the madeleine in the cup of tea has become, in the eyes of any Proust reader, the mythological moment of the Narrator's metamorphosis into a novelist holding at his disposal the story of his most enchanted years...

Let's add to those uncertainties quite a few others: there is little mention, for example, until the novel's famous ending, of the impact of aging on some of the main characters of a story that unfolds over forty years or more. Never do you get the impression that the beautiful Oriane de Guermantes, whom we regularly meet throughout the story, has changed from her early thirties (or late twenties) when the young Narrator falls in love with her, until her late sixties, or probably her seventies, at the princess's matinee. The same is true for Saint-Loup. As for the Narrator himself, he doesn't seem to be aware of his own age until the reactions of other guests at the Princesse de Guermantes's reception suddenly allow him to see the light: he too shows all the signs of age.

A more subtle remark about the immobility of time in the *Search* was indirectly suggested by Jacques Rivière in an article that he published on the novel: Rivière noticed, rightly so, the immobility of the Narrator's psychology. Proust took issue with this in a letter of January 15, 1920, to Jean de Pierrefeu (and that is how I know of the article): "Rivière gives too much the impression that my psychology...has something immobile (although he doesn't say it and doesn't find it)" (*Lettres*, 943, my translation). Indeed, think of the Narrator's mindset as presented throughout: it remains unchanged over some forty years...The character's psychology doesn't evolve, as if the impact of time did not exist.

Yet the passage of time and aging are recurrent themes in the Narrator's general reflections. Thus, in *Within a Budding Grove*, the adolescent, after pondering about our imperviousness to the movement of the earth, remarks that "so it is with Time in one's life. And to make its flight perceptible novelists are obliged, by wildly accelerating the beat of the pendulum, to transport the reader in a couple of minutes over ten, or twenty, or even thirty years. At the top of one page we have left a lover full of hope; at the foot of the next we meet him again, a bowed old man of eighty, painfully dragging himself on his daily walk around the courtyard of a hospital, scarcely replying to what is said to him, oblivious of the past. In saying of me, 'He's no longer a child,' 'His tastes won't change now,' and so forth, my father had suddenly made me conscious of myself in Time, and caused me the same kind of depression as if I had been, not yet the enfeebled old pensioner, but one of those heroes of whom the author, in a tone of indifference which is particularly galling, says to us at the end of a book: 'He very seldom comes up from the country now. He has finally decided to end his days there'" (*Search*, II, 74–75).

This apparent contradiction between the Narrator's abstract awareness of time and a rendition of the world that he observes and describes as mostly untouched by it is explained nowhere. It probably derives from a conception of time as an experience constantly brought to awareness, but that becomes objectified only when its manifestation in the outside world becomes unavoidable, such as in the terminal illness of others (as in the case of the grandmother, of Swann, or of Bergotte) and the sudden discovery of their extreme physical change, recognized after a long absence, and in one's own awareness of the reactions of others.

Jean-Yves Tadié mentions that Madame Verdurin must have been a hundred years old when she married the Prince de Guermantes after the death of her husband, a second brief marriage cut short by another death, as she had already ruled over her salon well before the Narrator's birth. Odette de Crecy, then Mme Swann, then Mme de Forcheville, is presented as the Duc de Guermantes's mistress at the matinee, although she met Swann and started their affair at the time of that early Verdurin salon. It's only some years after the matinee, at a reception that Gilberte de Saint-Loup organizes for the marriage of her own daughter, that some of the guests mention that the famous courtesan may not have all her marbles anymore...

The haziness of time indications gives a dreamlike quality to part of the narration, which contrasts with the extreme precision of the characters' behavior and words in their social life, although we don't perceive any hiatus between the one aspect and the other. There is, at first, a puzzling contradiction between the two domains, as *kairos*, the sacred moment of the sudden revelations of involuntary memory, is the very opposite of *kronos*, the measured time of daily chores and obligations, as well as that of social and political events. This contradiction doesn't apply to the remembrance of the Narrator's early life, but once his knife-sharp observations and knife-sharp irony about the social life that swirls around him and at times engulfs him come into play, there it is. Can dreamlike narration and social satire coexist? Manifestly they can within the time frame of the Narrator's story.

There may be many interpretations of this contradiction. Let me recall the suggestion offered at the end of the previous chapter: the Narrator moved, unconsciously, toward social life as a defense against the permanent anguish emanating from the never-forgotten sound of the pealing garden bell of his childhood; social life became for him the city noise of this dual metaphor, the noise that could for a time cover the sound of the convent bells. It's only late in life, when he discovered that he could become a writer, that the Narrator was able to discard a defense that would otherwise turn into an impediment, and see the continuity of his own existence as it would be revealed in the novel.

The impression of temporal immobility is bolstered by a peculiar structure of the novel: the centrality of repetition. The Narrator's most important amorous relation, with Albertine, is, as indicated by him, part of a chain of repetitions: "The [Duke de Guermantes's] liaison with Mme de Forcheville [Odette] had assumed such proportions that the old man, imitating in this final love the pattern of those he had had in the past, watched jealously over his mistress in a manner which, if my love for Albertine had, with important variations, repeated the love of Swann for Odette, made that of M. de Guermantes for this same Odette recall my own for Albertine" (*Search*, VI, 481).

More important, the very core of the novel, its social occasions, are repetitions of each other, only different according to the two classes portrayed: the upper bourgeoisie and the high aristocracy. In a period extending over many years, there are many almost-identical descriptions of dinners at the Verdurins' with almost the same guests throughout. Over the same length of time, we witness five almost-identical receptions at the highest aristocratic levels: at the Marquise de Saint-Euverte's, at the Marquise de Villeparisis's, at the Duchesse de Guermantes's and, twice, at the Princesse de Guermantes's.

Repetition's ability to create this immobility is enhanced by the constant presence, in the Narrator's consciousness and throughout his life, of the traumatic and defining event of his early childhood: the good-night kiss forced upon his mother, against her better judgment, which sought to impose some discipline to restrain the boy's extreme sensibility.

The "evening kiss" is the immobile trauma of the Narrator's life. Yet as we know, another event vies for first place, no less of an immobile memory, in the Narrator's life: the revelation, during these same childhood years in Combray, that his vocation is to become a writer.

Then, as time goes by, the negative comments by the much-admired Marquis de Norpois about his writings about Combray discourage him; his confidence is restored by Bergotte, but to no avail. Throughout successive stages of his life, we witness successive attempts to start writing and successive failures. "If only I had been able to start writing!" the Narrator, who has just returned to Paris from Doncières and Balbec and who is now probably in his twenties, admits. "What always emerged in the end from all my efforts was a virgin page, undefiled by any writing, ineluctable as that forced card which in certain tricks one invariably is made to draw, however carefully one may first have shuffled the pack" (*Search*, III, 196).

Like an oasis perceived by travelers in a desert, that hoped-for end point, that moment of true decision, moves out of reach whenever it's approached, until the last possible instant, when the aging Narrator, long away from

Paris, enters the courtyard of the Prince de Guermantes's mansion...

And that last possible moment isn't merely the one in which the Narrator discovers that he can and will be a writer after all, it is also the instant when the passage of time is revealed to him in its full impact and significance, at the Princesse de Guermantes's matinee, by its outward signs and by the sudden consciousness of his own mortality.

There may be few descriptions of death scenes in the *Search*, but the Narrator ponders about the unavoidable end in several particularly forceful, even anguished passages. The reader feels that, on this topic, the anxiety of the Narrator is a direct expression of the author, who remembers his mother's death, a few years later that of Agostinelli, and has to at some further stage confront his own approaching demise. The description of Bergotte's decline and death appears as an extraordinary expression of the author/Narrator's anxiety: anxiety about the end as such and about the significance of his own literary achievement in the face of that end. It is also a unique allusion to the possibility of an afterlife, a belief never stated by the author himself but that he allows the Narrator to convey.

Actually, although the Narrator expresses only once his belief in the possibility of an afterlife, he hesitates and contradicts himself several times in his belief about the fate of his writings. Sometimes, he despairs: "No doubt my books too, like my fleshly being, would in the end one day die. But death is a thing that we must resign ourselves to. We accept the thought that in ten years we ourselves, in a hundred years our books, will have ceased to exist. Eternal duration is promised no more to men's works than to men" (*Search*, VI, 524).

On other occasions, there is a glimmer of optimism regarding the fate of his writings. Thus, upon learning of Swann's death, the Narrator addresses him: "And yet, my dear Charles Swann, whom I used to know when I was still so young and you were nearing your grave, it is because he whom you must have regarded as a young idiot has made you the hero of one of his novels that people are beginning to speak of you again and that your name will perhaps live" (*Search*, V, 262). The most expansive and poetic expression of a belief in the afterlife of works concludes the comments upon Bergotte's death: "They buried him, but all through that night of mourning, in the lighted shop-windows, his books, arranged three by three, kept vigil like angels with outspread wings and seemed, for him who was no more, the symbol of his resurrection." It is just before that evocation of the possible perennial existence of some writings that the Narrator declared: "The idea that Bergotte was not dead for ever is by no means improbable" (*Search*, V, 246).

We all know that, regarding the afterlife of writings, the Narrator was both wrong and right: Anatole France is forgotten; Marcel Proust lives.

Ultimately, though, it was the death of his "fleshly being" that weighed foremost on the mind of the Narrator: his own self's death, either sudden or long drawn out. The survival of his writings was the corollary: would he live long enough to write what he had to write?

The Narrator introduces his rumination about death, so central to the thoughts that weigh on him at the princess's matinee, by the few words he exchanges with Charlus during their brief encounter on the Champs-Elysées. Charlus is proud of still being alive, after a massive stroke: "[It] was with an almost triumphal sternness that he repeated, in a monotonous tone ... and with a dull sepulchral resonance: 'Hannibal de Bréauté, dead! Antoine de Mouchy, dead! Charles Swann, dead! Adalbert de Montmorency, dead! Boson de Talleyrand, dead! Sosthène de Doudeauville, dead!' And every time he uttered it, the word 'dead' seemed to fall upon his departed friends like a spadeful of earth each heavier than the last, thrown by a grave-digger grimly determined to immure them yet more closely within the tomb" (*Search*, VI, 249). The grim gravedigger who follows the grim reaper.

Death, the Narrator reflects, can be totally unexpected: "We may, indeed, say that the hour of death is uncertain, but when we say this we think of that hour as situated in a vague and remote expanse of time; it does not occur to us that it can have any connexion with the day that has already dawned ... [death] may occur this very afternoon, so far from uncertain, this afternoon whose timetable, hour by hour, has been settled in advance" (*Search*, III, 427). The death of the mother is rapid, that of Agostinelli is sudden, accidental, unforeseeable.

Sudden death may not be the worst. It is the slow progression of death, visible in signs of terminal illness and of the physical decay caused by old age, suddenly noticed by those close and loving, that may be hardly endurable for them. Thus, the Narrator, just back in Balbec from a stay at Doncières, where his friend Saint-Loup is stationed during his military service, comes upon his beloved grandmother, who did not yet expect him and had not noticed his presence in their drawing room. "Suddenly, in our drawing-room which formed part of a new world, that of Time, that which is inhabited by the strangers of whom we say 'He's begun to age a good deal,' for the first time and for a moment only, since she vanished very quickly, I saw, sitting on the sofa beneath the lamp, red-faced, heavy and vulgar, sick, day-dreaming, letting her slightly crazed eyes wander over a book, an overburdened old woman whom I didn't know" (Search, III, 185).

These experiences of death, of one's time (or that of a beloved person) brutally cut short, merge in the anxious mind of the Narrator with the possibility, once he is set on starting to write, that the time needed to complete his work may not be granted to him: "In my awareness of the approach of death I resembled a dying soldier, and like him too, before I died, I had something to write. But my task was longer than his, my words had to reach more than a single person . . . And I should live in the anxiety of not knowing whether the master of my destiny might not prove less indulgent than the Sultan Shahriyar [in The Arabian Nights]" (Search, VI, 524).

Life for the Narrator, from that moment on, becomes a constant obsession with death: "The idea of death took up permanent residence within me ... its image adhered now to the most profound layer of my mind, so completely that I could not give my attention to anything without that thing first traversing the idea of death, and even if no object occupied my attention and I remained in a state of complete repose, the idea of death still kept me company as faithfully as the idea of my self" (*Search*, VI, 523).

The fear of dying before being able to complete his novel was undoubtedly a constant worry for the Narrator, the more so that illness constantly stalked him. Yet, the readiness to discuss death but to limit its full-length description to the grandmother's final days brings us back to the mother's death. There may have been resentment in the Narrator's decision to avoid any evocation of Mamma's passing away, but there could also have been filial piety in this avoidance: How could the author/Narrator describe in any detail the final moments of the only true love of his life?

.8.

MEMORY

n Search is a paean to memory. Although the novel is in part turned toward the future in a constant expectation of the "true" decision to start writing, this decision itself, as we know, comes suddenly, when the Narrator experiences, as he steps on the uneven stones in the courtyard of the Prince de Guermantes's mansion, an epiphany of involuntary memory, a revelation, no longer expected, of his ability to be a creative writer. The memory of the Saint Mark's baptistery in Venice, evoked by the uneven stones, indicates that it is in past events, retrieved in bursts of memory, that the future literary creation will find its material. It will be a remembrance of things past, forgotten and suddenly retrieved.

A contradiction that seems to have escaped the Narrator resides in the incompatibility between "search" (*recherche*), a purposive action, an active undertaking, and involuntary memory, which cannot be the result of a voluntary undertaking. Further on, I will return to this fundamental contradiction and to its consequences. Beforehand, it's necessary to take a closer look at the Narrator's constantly mentioned concept.

I must admit not being clear about the point in Proust's writings at which memory—and, particularly, involuntary memory—became a fundamental concept. Funnily enough, in "The Confession of a Young Woman," the young woman calls the village to which she is brought by her mother, year-in, year-out, to spend apparently long vacations, Les Oublis (Oblivions); in the *Search* this village becomes Combray (*Pleasures and Days*, 106). Was that intentional well before the call for the great novel ever came?

What may be meant by involuntary memory? At the outset, when Proust starts writing down thoughts in his 1908 notebook, thoughts that will lead to sketches subsequently becoming sequences in the *Search*, he remarks: "We consider the past as being mediocre because we think it, but the past is not that, it is rather the unevenness of pavements in the Saint Mark's baptistery (photograph of the St. Mark Repose, which we didn't have in mind anymore[)]" (Proust, *Carnets*, 49, my translation).

It appears, therefore, that what Proust favored from the outset was a rejection of intellectual attempts to retrieve the past, choosing instead the evocative power of a sensation that didn't suddenly bring back past events but a memory of such events mediated by the sight of a photograph. This early evocation of a sensual mode of remembrance doesn't seem to have had yet any major function in the author's thoughts about his future work.

The perception just mentioned was an early step toward the recognition of a process much closer to what will become involuntary memory. Much has been written about Proustian memory, but I am not sure that what the author and Narrator meant gives us a clear picture: their definitions are not always identical, and even the Narrator's interpretations are not always the same.

The most encompassing definition of Proust's notion of memory is possibly that offered by Walter Benjamin: "An experienced event is finite—at any rate, confined to one sphere of experience; a remembered event is infinite, because it is only a key to everything that happened before it and after it" (Benjamin, "The Image of Proust," 202). Such a wide definition of "remembered events" excludes in fact any criticism of involuntary memory.

There is, at the other end of the spectrum, a definition that at first glance makes much sense. For Geneviève Henrot, involuntary memory has to carry the following four features: "the sensation itself, the passive condition of the receiver, the process of remembering, and the past event relived" (Henrot, 107). What is recognized here is certainly at the core of involuntary memory. Henrot discovered about a hundred such examples of involuntary memory in the *Search* and in drafts for the novel.

Let me quote one such example offered by the Narrator: "What best reminds us of a person is precisely what we had forgotten (because it was of no importance, and we therefore left it in full possession of its strength). That is why the better part of our memories exists outside us, in a blatter of rain, in the smell of an unaired room or of the first crackling brushwood fire in a cold grate: wherever, in short, we happen upon what our mind, having no use for it, had rejected, the last treasure that the past has in store, the richest, that which, when all our flow of tears seems to have dried at the source, can make us weep again. Outside us? Within us, rather, but hidden from our eyes in an oblivion more or less prolonged" (*Search*, II, 300).

Two remarks come to mind. First, such general and often-felt sensations are very unlikely reminders of a long-forgotten person; thus, second, for a sensory experience to trigger involuntary memory, it has to be, usually, very specifically linked to the forgotten person or event, like Aunt Léonie's madeleine dipped in a cup of tea. In short, in the above-mentioned example, the Narrator offers a mistaken illustration of involuntary memory, and Geneviève Henrot ought to add the specificity of the trigger as a further necessary criterion.

In fact, from the very outset the notion of involuntary memory presents quite a few problems. Thus, the "evening kiss" scene and all the events that led to it have rightly been considered traumatic, and according to the Narrator's own testimony, moments that resonated throughout his adult life, as we saw. Why then would the Narrator have needed, sometime during those same later years, the madeleine dipped in a cup of tea that his mother had prepared for him on a cold and rainy day to remember suddenly, unexpectedly, involuntarily, the blissful days of his childhood vacations in Combray, when among so many other wonderful things his aunt Léonie offered him every Sunday morning the same kind of delicious madeleine, dipped in a cup of tea?

The Narrator answers this obvious question rather dismissively: "I must own that I could have assured any questioner that Combray did include other scenes and did exist at other hours than these. But since the facts which I should then have recalled would have been prompted only by voluntary memory, the memory of the intellect, and since the pictures which that kind of memory shows us preserve nothing of the past itself, I should never have had any wish to ponder over this residue of Combray. To me it was in reality all dead" (Search, I, 59). The answer is far from convincing Regarding the Narrator's unlikely amnesia, one could offer two answers. First, the Narrator could not base his sunny remembrance of Combray on a traumatic event; a happy, sensual moment was needed to bring back those enchanted days; secondly, the Narrator needed the notion of involuntary memory as a sort of epiphany to establish the unexpected recognition of his creative literary powers and to finally start writing. But as we saw in the previous chapter, it seems more than doubtful that the cup of tea had any immediate writing sequel...

Could one not say, in order to solve this mystery, that in all these cases (the uneven stones, the cup of tea, etc.), the epiphanies were merely wonderful literary devices left to the Narrator and recognized as such by the author as the writing of *Search* progressed?

And yet, Proust seemed to attach some real creative importance to involuntary memory, both in his notations in the *Carnets* and in his correspondence, that went beyond the function of a simple device. He does so, for example, in the letter of early November 1913 to René Blum, a friend of his first publisher, Bernard Grasset, a letter that I mentioned in the introduction. There, he reasserts his belief that this specific form of memory is "the only true one," the only one that can offer us an authentic rendition of the past. And he refers again to the madeleine sequence as illustrating the resurgence of "part of my life that I had forgotten" (*Lettres*, 636–37).

We have also references to the importance of such memory in the *Carnets* of the same period, the most explicit of which appears in "Carnet 3," covering approximately the year 1914: "Should not forget that there is a theme which comes back in my life which is even more important than Albertine's love...it is the theme of remembrance, the stuff of artistic creation (cup of tea, trees on a walk, church steeples, etc.)" (*Carnets*, 327–28). The impression left by this notation is that the author is reminding himself not to forget this essential conceptual backbone...We have returned again to the notion of a literary device.

Actually, once Proust decided that involuntary memory was the essential foundation for the Narrator's story, he attempted to save it even where the task was almost impossible. Thus, in the second part of *Swann's Way*, "Swann in Love," the events it evokes took place before the Narrator's birth, and every aspect of which was supposedly told to him by an unidentified person; the details could not, by definition, be brought back by a sudden revelation. At some point, the Narrator tries to explain away that basic impossibility, but he merely offers beautiful metaphors, or so it seems to me:

> Thus would I often lie until morning, dreaming of the old days of Combray, of my melancholy and wakeful evenings there, of other days besides, the memory of which had been more recently restored to me by the taste...of a cup of tea, and, by an association of memories, of a story which, many years after I had left the little place, have been told me of a love affair in which Swann had been involved before I was born, with a precision of details which it is often easier to obtain for the lives of people who have been dead for centuries than for those of our own most intimate friends, an accuracy which it seems as impossible to attain as it seemed impossible to speak from one town to another, before we knew of the contrivance by which that impossibility has been overcome. All these memories, superimposed upon one another, now formed a single mass, but had

not so far coalesced that I could not discern between them—between my oldest, my instinctive memories, and those others, inspired more recently by a taste or "perfume," and finally those which were actually the memories of another person from whom I had acquired them at second hand—if not real fissures, real geological faults, at least that veining, that variegation of colouring, which in certain rocks, in certain blocks of marble, points to differences of origin, age, and formation. (*Search*, I, 262).

Proust must have smiled when he allowed his Narrator to take the telephone as one metaphor and blocks of marble as the other one in a courageous effort to illustrate how different kinds of involuntary memory inspired his remembrance of things past, even when they dealt with the words, the feelings, the thoughts and the initiatives of characters involved in events that took place before the Narrator was born. In short, it could well be that Combray, the memory of Combray, arose suddenly from the "perfume" of a cup of tea, but, although the inspiring and creative dimensions of such a memory are convincing when applied to the "melancholy and wakeful evenings" of that time, most of the Narrator's reminiscences were necessarily founded on intelligent, rational, memory retrieval—that roundly dismissed involuntary memory— and, only at times on the Narrator's poetic imagination.

Take the entire social tapestry unfolded in the novel: it was necessarily a reconstruction performed by intelligent memory. The Narrator knows this, recognizes it, and yet tries to brush it off. Here he is, leaving a reception at the Duchesse de Guermantes's, a reception during which the conversations of hosts and guests are reported in a monumental narration of well over a hundred pages. "When all was said," the Narrator writes, "the stories I had heard at Mme de Guermantes's, very different in this respect from what I had felt in the case of the hawthorns, or when I tasted a *madeleine*, remained alien to me. Entering me for a moment and possessing me only physically, it was as though, being of a social, not an individual nature, they were impatient to escape.... In the meantime they made my lips quiver as I stammered them to myself, and I tried in vain to bring back and concentrate a mind that was carried away by a centrifugal force" (*Search*, III, 756). Remarkably, though, the Narrator remembered verbatim those miles and miles of stories held merely in the cusp of voluntary memory. Let's add that no epiphany could reveal the manifold layers of Baron de Charlus's personality nor, a fortiori, of his conversations or, of his secret—and not so secret—life. No involuntary memory could bring back the tiniest details of the long and tortuous love affair between the Narrator and Albertine, either.

What could have been the intellectual influences on Proust's notion of involuntary memory? Freud? Bergson? It seems that there was no direct influence of Freud on Proust, nor of Bergson on Proust (though they knew each other, as Bergson had married Proust's cousin, and Marcel was best man at the wedding). Actually, regarding Bergson, Tadié mentions a remark of the philosopher in a letter to Henri Massis, who quoted it in 1937: "Essentially, [Proust's] way of thinking was very much inclined to turn its back on duration and the life force" which were Bergson's two major concepts; this remark, according to Tadié, clearly shows the cool relations between the two men (Tadié, *Proust*, 270).

In the case of Freud, some relation, specifically about memory and the unconscious, may seem relevant, but only at first glance. In a letter of September 11, 1921, to Roger Allard, who had published a review of *The Guermantes Way* in the *NRF*, an ever-suspicious Proust declared that he didn't understand a reference to Sigmund Freud, as he hadn't read him and wondered whether the allusion was negative in any way. In fact, in his very positive review, Allard had merely made the following reference to *The Interpretation of Dreams*: "Following Professor Freud, a school considers dream as an effort of the physical being to fulfill a hidden desire by offering it a symbolic substitute. One may agree that all artistic creation is the product of a similar desire. Thus considered, it gets rid of the false motivations that the author generally likes to attribute to it and appears under a different guise. Following M. Proust's simple and profound sentence: 'It is reason that opens our eyes,' one could say that the refutation of an error grants us an additional signification" (*Lettres*, 1031–32, my translation).

There is nonetheless a basic common awareness shared by Freud and Proust: the recognition of the decisive importance of unconscious motivations in human behavior. But the conclusions each of them draws from these premises are entirely different, even contrary. Whereas for Freud the repressed, unconscious memory of some traumatic event will remain hidden but active in triggering neurotic symptoms and will be uncovered only by a rational investigation applied to its manifestations by the cooperation of analyst and patient, Proust's involuntary memory is not disruptive while hidden and cannot be brought to light by rational investigation; it will surge to consciousness only as a result of the haphazard impact of a physical sensation producing an unexpected chain of associations, leading to the sudden awareness of a similar sensation in a moment of past life, forgotten until then.

Some commentators have mentioned the influence of Schopenhauer and of some French psychologists, contemporaries of Proust: Theodule Ribot, Pierre Janet, Alfred Brissaud (Jack Jordan, "The Unconscious," *Cambridge Companion*, 102). All of this is beyond the reach of this essay.

When did Proust recognize the importance of involuntary memory for his forthcoming novel? I don't know of any clear answer to this question. As the author started writing down notes for his novel in the 1908 notebook, he included the memory of the Saint Mark's baptistry, as we saw, but didn't give it any centrality. On the other hand, in *Jean Santeuil*, written at least ten years before, there are several allusions to involuntary resurgences of the past that seem essential for a poetic, truly literary, rendition of similar events in the narration of the present (*Jean Santeuil*, 462–63 et al.).

One additional definition of involuntary memory from the Narrator may be helpful. "Let a noise or a scent, once heard or once smelt, be heard or smelt again in the present and at the same time in the past, real without being actual, ideal without being abstract, and immediately the permanent and habitually concealed essence of things is liberated and our true self, which seemed—had perhaps for long years seemed—to be dead but was not altogether dead, is awakened and reanimated as it receives the celestial nourishment that is brought to it. A minute freed from the order of time has re-created in us, to feel it, the man freed from the order of time. And one can understand that this man should have confidence in his joy, even if the simple taste of a madeleine does not seem logically to contain within it the reasons for this joy, one can understand that the word 'death' should have no meaning for him; situated outside time, why should he fear the future?" (*Search*, VI, 264–65).

Previously, the Narrator had evoked some of the main occasions on which a sudden sensation brought back to him the involuntary memory of episodes belonging to a long-forgotten past: "Suddenly . . . a marvelous expedient of nature . . . had caused a sensation . . . to be mirrored at one and the same time in the past, so that my imagination was permitted to savour it, and in the present, where the actual shock to my senses of the noise [of the hammer], the touch of the linen napkin, or whatever it might be, had added to the dreams of the imagination the concept of 'existence' which they usually lack, and through this subterfuge had made it possible for my being to secure, to isolate, to immobilise— for a moment brief as a flash of lightning—what normally it never apprehends: a fragment of time in the pure state" (*Search*, VI, 263–64).

These are strong words indeed, and the possible influence of Plato's philosophy on Proust is not as far-fetched as some commentators have argued, although it is more likely, given the very emphasis of the words, that they express the Narrator's own feelings, experiences, and ideas. And, beyond this "flash of lightning," there is a question that haunts the Narrator: What is the process he, then, needs to follow in order to move from personal illumination to literary creation? "Certain comparisons which are false if we start from them as premises may well be true if we arrive at them as conclusions. The man of letters envies the painter, he would like to take notes and make sketches, but it is disastrous for him to do so. Yet when he writes, there is not a single gesture of his characters, not a trick of behaviour, not a tone of voice which has not been supplied to his inspiration by his memory...And in the end the writer realises that if his dream of being a sort of painter was not in a conscious and intentional manner capable of fulfilment, it has nevertheless been fulfilled and that he too, for his work as a writer, has unconsciously made use of a sketch-book. For, impelled by the instinct that was in him, the writer, long before he thought that he would one day become one, regularly omitted to look at a great many things which other people notice...but all this time he was instructing his eyes and his ears to retain for ever what seemed to others puerile trivialities, the tone of voice in which a certain remark had been made...[This] tone of voice was one that he had heard before or felt that he might hear again, because it was something renewable, durable. There is a feeling for generality which, in the future writer, itself picks out what is general and can for that reason one day enter into a work of art" (*Search*, VI, 305–6).

The "tone of voice" (offered here as just one example among several others)—one retained by the future writer because of the sense of generality attached to it—is later recaptured by the same instinctive recognition of its general character and intuitively used in the literary work of art.

One sidenote: In Proust's February 1914 letter to Jacques Rivière, mentioned above, there are a few lines relevant to our quarry: "It is only at the end of the book, and once the lessons of life have been understood, that my thinking will become manifest. What I express at the end of my first volume...is the contrary of my conclusion [only the first volume had been published by 1914, but we know that Proust had already a clear idea of the end of the novel]. It is merely a stage, in appearance subjective and dilettante, leading to the most objective and believing of conclusions...In this first volume you saw the pleasure that the taste of the madeleine dipped in tea gave me, I say that I am not feeling mortal anymore, etc. and that I don't know why. I will explain it only at the end of the third volume [at the time Proust planned only three volumes]. Everything is built that way...If I didn't have any intellectual convictions, if I was simply attempting at remembering and at duplicating the days of my life with these memories, I wouldn't, ill as I am, make the effort of writing. But I didn't want to analyze abstractly this evolution of a mind [*l'évolution d'une pensée*], I wanted to re-create it, to make it live again" (Proust, *Lettres*, 667, my translation).

In other words, we find here the fundamental notion present in all of the Narrator's descriptions of involuntary memory: remembrance, to be creative, should not be solely a recapturing of the images of past events but should also carry the reexperiencing of the sensations and emotions that were previously linked to them to the point of reliving that past. What Proust alluded to in his letter to Rivière—and what the Narrator mentions in each description of the epiphanies of involuntary memory—is a sudden sense of all-suffusing joy, of feeling liberated from time, of feeling immortal. This element, inherent to the author's and Narrator's sense of involuntary memory, was also missing from Henrot's presentation of its necessary components. There is moreover the need to rework the immediate experience, to generalize, in order to create the true work of literary art.

The two faces of memory, the illumination and the generalization, cannot and need not be linked: the first has given us Combray, Balbec, Venice, and episodes of Paris life, of the great love sequences and, possibly, the last matinee at the Princesse de Guermantes's; without the second, we wouldn't have the entire social tapestry of the novel, the Indian summer of its aristocracy, the victorious ascension of its upper middle class, the colorful world of its servants, the equivocal one of its inverts and of its Jews. It seems to me that the puzzle stemming from the inadequacy of involuntary memory for addressing the novel's social world has been solved; the Narrator, under the guise of generalizing memory, has accepted the function of its voluntary face for that part of the novel.

Yet, these two faces of memory may have come close to each other in the stunning portraits the Narrator traces of his important figures, also of the less important ones and, equally, of the unimportant bit players, portraits born of attitudes and conversations, sometimes just rendered by striking metaphors (remember Monsieur de Palancy). Close together? Maybe not in all portraits. Swann is not typical, Baron de Charlus is not typical, and maybe Saint-Loup is not either, even if the three characters owe something to Proust's contemporaries. A few of the figures of *In Search* that have become literary icons were not created out of generalities, and generalities cannot encompass them. A writer's genius may be fed by memory, but it owes the most to imagination.

We have already discussed the difficulties regarding any major use of the epiphanies of involuntary memory in the creation of *In Search* and, in particular, the reminder that the author put in his Notebook 3 about having to keep in mind that this was the fundamental constituent of the novel (even more, he stated, than the love for Albertine). This confirms that the contradiction between the title of the novel and the notion of involuntary memory, albeit probably not perceived by Proust, shows that from the outset, involuntary memory was nothing else but a magnificent literary device, one to be remembered...

Albertine was dead. "I had now only one hope left for the future—" the distressed Narrator says, "a hope far more poignant than any fear—and that was that I might forget Albertine. I knew that I should forget her one day; I had forgotten Gilberte and Mme de Guermantes; I had forgotten my grandmother. And it is our most just and cruel punishment for that forgetfulness... through which we have detached ourselves from those we no longer love, that we should recognise it to be inevitable in the case of those we love still. In reality, we know that it is not a painful state but a state of indifference." (Search, V, 650). For the time being, the Narrator whistles in the night to find some courage, but of course he is right regarding the future.

It is always amusing to follow the Narrator along, up to his unavoidable contradictions. After all, life is full of contradictions... Nonetheless, how can we reconcile our guide's certainty about forgetting even those we love most and the ever-present pealing of the garden bell, the ever-present love between the Narrator and his mother?

More generally, the Narrator's theory of automatic forgetting doesn't seem to apply to his Mamma's lasting love for her own mother (the Narrator's grandmother), even if *he* had forgotten her. All in all, it doesn't make the notion of involuntary memory easier to use, as sudden epiphanies can only apply to very superficially forgotten events. In short, if we rely on the Narrator's theory of memory, we may only reassert that although Proust was possibly the greatest French poet in prose, he wasn't much of a thinker as far as the conceptual infrastructure of *In Search* goes. But who cares?

CONCLUDING REMARKS AND SOME MORE

Each of us, *In Search* readers, returns to some haunting episodes again and again, and for each of us they may be different. But at some stage we all have to make an effort to remember that it's not Proust's story that we follow but that of his Narrator. And yet we sense that as we are enthralled by the unfolding of that life's description, we recognize a deep layer of authenticity. We can even identify what the author doesn't want to tell us, or, some other time, what he doesn't want to tell but hopes that some readers will uncover. It is on that search of the *Search* that this essay is based. Of course, many questions raised in our text have remained unanswered, but hopefully at least a few may have received some further emphasis.

First, as this essay was meant to offer a closer look at some of the author's traits and choices by focusing on the Narrator's statements and equivocations, let me mention again a few of the characteristics that have been stressed here. In his essay on Proust, subtitled "The Fictions of Life and Art," Leo Bersani pointed to Marcel's weakness of self and his need for the outside world to fill a never-satiated sense of emptiness. This all-encompassing trait is well described and could be seen as the foundation of those more concrete aspects that I attempted to clarify, namely the author/Narrator's start of *In Search* as the resolution of the conflicting feelings toward the mother, and after her disappearance, his inability to come to terms with one major component of his identity: his Jewishness. There is no doubt that he came to terms with his homosexuality, but as we saw he probably worried about his readers' potential reactions, hence the homophobic rant he introduced in the last additional volume of the novel. The preceding volumes were nonetheless clear enough.

The author's relentless social climbing (before he knew that it would vastly enrich *In Search*), bolstered by sycophantic flattery as shown in his letters and his unwavering friendship with the very anti-Semitic Alphonse and Léon Daudet and with the unbearable Paul Morand, finds its reflections in the novel: there, as in reality, we follow the Narrator's social acrobatics and we soon discover that hostility to Jews does not seem to have had any impact on him or on Swann's personal relations. In general, I admit that, for me, the Narrator does not awaken much sympathy, nor does the personality of Marcel Proust, from what one knows of him. But, as André Gide once quipped, *"les bons sentiments ne font pas de la bonne littérature"* ("good sentiments do not make for good literature"). We read *In Search* for *"la bonne littérature."*

Is *In Search* a modern novel? I know that this issue is at the core of Antoine Compagnon's excellent study *Proust entre deux siècles*, mentioned above, but our arguments are entirely different, and so are our conclusions.

Several aspects of the novel should be taken into account. On one hand, *Search* can be seen as an immense bildungsroman, where at the outset the young Narrator's gift for writing is presented as question and aspiration, a question and an aspiration that will find their positive answer at the very end of the novel, while the intervening chapters are the slow learning process and the accumulation of experience that will ultimately allow the final epiphany. Such a definition may be considered as a somewhat extended perception of the genre, but cannot be rejected. It offers the first element of an answer to the question of modernity and looks negative. The bildungsroman is a venerable genre whose very august ancestry leads us at least to Goethe. Any novel partaking of it, even if the "education" described takes place in modern times and includes modern ideas, follows a traditional pattern, be it in the case of Thomas Mann's *Magic Mountain* or in that of Proust's novel. The education can take seven years, as for Hans Castorp, the hero of *The Magic Mountain*, or forty years, as for the Narrator in the *Search*, but it is an education nonetheless.

And then there is the style of the novel. Proust's *In Search* is probably the most magnificent example of traditional French style in a novel, but it remains traditional notwithstanding its poetic splendor; there is no attempt in it to experiment with new forms of narration or of style. The opposite can be said of a contemporaneous novel: James Joyce's *Ulysses*, of course.

Finally, I have previously mentioned that the absence of ugliness and of Evil (except for snippets of ugliness as a foil for the vastly dominant beauty) also put in question the modernity of *In Search*. This is not necessarily a sine qua non condition, but linked to the two other traditionalist dimensions, it confirms one possible conclusion: Proust's great novel, as magnificent as it is, cannot be considered modern. Indeed, it is part of a tradition that flourished and continues to flourish, possibly more than literary creations that are considered epitomes of modernity. Jacques Rivière put it exactly right in the very title of the article he published in February 1920 in the *NRF*: "Marcel Proust et la tradition classique."

That was "on the one hand." The other aspect is obvious: The setting, at the center of the novel, of *Sodom and Gomorrah* was unusual for its time (notwithstanding Gide's contribution) and remains rare, even today, in mainstream literature. This turns *In Search* into a very modern novel indeed.

What would be one of the Narrator's most unpalatable statements?" Why ask such a question? The reason is simple:

all through this study, I followed the Narrator's lapses in order to better understand the author and the text as such; it makes sense, therefore, to end the essay with an issue of major significance along that line of inquiry.

I will quote the Narrator on two apparently distinct matters that nonetheless could be related. The first matter is a reminder of what has already been discussed: the comparison of Bloch to a hyena. I mentioned the unusually brutal aspect of the comparison and the fact that the Narrator adopted it intentionally, as he used it twice, in all its details, in different parts of the story, separated by some twenty years in terms of the narration. Now, this comparison, possibly the most offensive one among the hundreds of those applied to characters throughout the entire novel, is particularly weird, as Bloch, a school friend, is never reported as having intentionally caused any harm to the Narrator, except for embarrassing him in high society by his lack of social savoir faire and his uncouthness. In short, Bloch, the "little Jew," whose only crime is social climbing, until he achieves some eminence thanks to his writing and his erudition, becomes the emblem of what the Narrator hates most, as it is so close to his secret self-image: the ascension of a Jew in a society that will never fully accept him as one of its own. It is a cruel fact that dawned on Swann only when he became terminally ill, and must have been perceived by the author throughout the many years of his own climbing while still being Marcel. "I chatted for a minute or two with Swann," writes the Narrator, meeting his old friend at the penultimate reception at the Princess de Guermantes's, "...and asked him how it was that all the Guermantes were anti-Dreyfusards. 'In the first place because at heart all these people are anti-semites,' replied Swann" (*Search*, III, 796).

The second matter was only briefly discussed previously; it is the Narrator's evocation and mainly his comments on sadism. Much before the pseudo-sadism encountered in Jupien's brothel, one encounters what appears as true sadism in the ritual profanation of Vinteuil's memory by his cherished daughter and her lesbian friend, when during their love game they spit upon the dead musician's photograph. It is in evoking that scene that the Narrator offers an apologia for the sort of sadism practiced by Vinteuil's daughter in order to achieve the pleasure she cannot achieve otherwise. "A sadist of her kind is an artist in evil, which a wholly wicked person could not be, for in that case the evil would not have been external, it would have seemed quite natural to her, and would not even have been distinguishable from herself; and as for virtue, respect for the dead, filial affection, since she would never have practised the cult of these things, she would take no impious delight in profaning them. Sadists of Mlle Vinteuil's sort are creatures so purely sentimental, so naturally virtuous, that even sensual pleasure appears to them as something bad, the prerogative of the wicked. And when they allow themselves for a moment to enjoy it they endeavour to impersonate, to identify with, the wicked, and to make their partners do likewise, in order to gain the momentary illusion of having escaped beyond the control of their own gentle and scrupulous natures into the inhuman world of pleasure. And I could understand how she must have longed for such an escape when I saw how impossible it was for her to effect it" (*Search*, I, 231).

The Narrator's comments lead immediately to an almost obvious association: this is the interpretation of and the excuse for the author's own sadistic rituals, those he avowed to André Gide, namely that, at times, in order to achieve orgasm he needed to watch two starved rats tearing at each other inside a cage. (As I indicated, no proof exists to believe that this passage was also an interpretation and an excuse for the oft-mentioned identical desecration of the memory of the author's mother, in the brothel he patronized, where, supposedly, similar spitting rituals took place.)

The Narrator's interpretation indicates in any case that a symbolic act of desecration opens the gates to a relief that otherwise cannot be achieved. That sadistic gesture has to be directed at an innocent being—and only at an innocent being—in order to relieve the would-be sadist of a paralyzing taboo. And, if so, whom did the Narrator wish to relieve, be it fictionally, of a hated Jewish identity, by hurling twice the most brutal invective at his friend Bloch, if not the author himself?

When I tried to explain in the introduction what made me choose Proust as the subject of this essay, I mentioned my musings about memory and identity, about my own identity and my own memory. Had I been a literary scholar, no question would have been asked, but a historian of the Holocaust, who has no competence and no intention of becoming another Proust specialist, has to explain his choice. I see, first, a rather superficial reason, that should, nonetheless, be noted.

Soon after arriving in France from Prague, in 1939, and entering grade school, first near Paris, then in Néris-les-Bains, in 1940, I became totally French and totally enraptured by a language that remained my main language for the rest of my life. Thus, when choosing my second literary topic ("Kafka" had brought me back to my place of birth and to many reminders of my family), I quite naturally turned to the most admirable French novelist, whom over the following years and decades I read and reread (for the first time, it was probably at the Lycée Henri-IV, in early 1947, but probably only the first volume). Thus, although moving officially from one identity to the next, I was affirming to myself that culturally I was and remained French (even though this essay has been written in English...).

The second reason had not occurred to me until I started writing these pages, but then it became increasingly plausible. Throughout my life, I haven't remembered the pealing of any garden bell, nor did I recall any sobs, as happened to the Narrator, but just an immense pain that as a memory never left me: the memory of my last meeting with my mother and my father, at the age of ten, in the hospital room in Montlucon where they were hiding, in September 1942.

All of that never occurred to me as a reason for writing about Proust's *Recherche*, but maybe this was it. This is it.

How does one take leave of an essay on Proust? I would like to offer to the reader an excerpt of *In Search* that does not belong to the standard anthology pieces, which are usually more exuberant but also too well known by now, and that, as one among hundreds, conveys the supreme beauty of a style, here fusing both vision and sound, that even translation kept pristine. Young Marcel, anguished by the thought that the presence of Swann at the dinner table will deprive him of his mother's good-night kiss, opens the window of his room: "Outside, things too seemed frozen, rapt in a mute intentness not to disturb the moonlight which, duplicating each of them and throwing it back by the extension in front of it of a shadow denser and more concrete than its substance, had made the whole landscape at once thinner and larger, like a map which, after being folded up, is spread out upon the ground. What had to move—a leaf of the chestnut tree, for instance—moved. But its minute quivering, total, self-contained, finished down to its minutest gradation and its last delicate tremor, did not impinge upon the rest of the scene, did not merge with it, remained circumscribed. Exposed upon this surface of silence which absorbed nothing of them, the most distant sounds, those which must have come from gardens at the far end of the town, could be distinguished with such exact 'finish' that the impression they gave of coming from a distance seemed due only to their 'pianissimo' execution, like those movements on muted strings so well performed by the orchestra of the Conservatoire that, even though one does not miss a single note, one thinks none the less that they are being played somewhere outside, a long way from the concert hall..." (*Search*, I, 43).

The Narrator doesn't leave it at that; the sentence ends with an enigma: "...so that all the old subscribers—my grandmother's sisters too, when Swann had given them his seats—used to strain their ears as if they had caught the distant approach of an army on the march, which had not yet rounded the corner of the Rue de Trévise." The mysterious army belongs to a local garrison; at times, and it always creates much excitement among Combray's inhabitants, it marches through the streets of the town on its way to some exercise. The enigma is elsewhere: the grandmother's two sisters, Céline and Flora, did not leave Combray, and they display something of the limitations of the local inhabitants; their rootedness in the village hints at something that the Narrator argues about later in the novel and that I discussed at length: the mother's own roots in the village, in other words her local ascendance. But doesn't this contradict the grandmother's very different spirit, values, and education and her living in Paris, as does the mother? In short, Jewish or not? And what then about the grandmother's sisters? The Narrator seems confused, possibly unable to decide, as confused as the author himself, and as is this commentator: in short, Proustian uncertainties.

BIBLIOGRAPHY

MARCEL PROUST

Carnets. Edited by Florence Callu and Antoine Compagnon. Paris: Gallimard, 2002.

In Search of Lost Time. Translated by C. K. Scott Moncrieff, Terence Kilmartin, and Andreas Mayor. Revised by D. J. Enright, and with an introduction by Richard Howard. 6 vols. New York: Modern Library, 2003.

Jean Santeuil. Édition de Pierre Clarac et Yves Sandre avec la collaboration de Jean Yves Tadié. Préface de Jean Yves Tadié. Quarto. Paris: Gallimard, 2001.

Le mystérieux correspondant et autres nouvelles inédites. Suivi de "Aux sources de la *Recherche du temps perdu*." Textes transcrits, annotés et présentés par Luc Fraisse. Paris: Éditions de Fallois, 2019.

Letters to His Neighbor. Translated by Lydia Davis. Foreword by Jean-Yves Tadié. New York: New Directions, 2017.

Lettres. Paris: Éditions Plon, 2004.

Marcel Proust on Art and Literature, 1896–1919. Translated and edited by Sylvia Townsend Warner. Introduction by Terence Kilmartin. New York: Carroll & Graf, 1984.

Pleasures and Days. Translated by Andrew Brown. Foreword by A. N. Wilson. Richmond, Surrey: Alma Classics, 2013.

OTHER WORKS

Albaret, Céleste. Monsieur Proust: Souvenirs recueillis par Georges Belmont. Paris: Robert Laffont, 1973.

Bataille, Georges. "Marcel Proust et la mère profanée." *Critique* 1, no. 47 (December 1946): 601–11.

Benjamin, Walter. "The Image of Proust." In *Illuminations*, translated by Harry Zohn, edited and with an introduction by Hannah Arendt, 201–16. New York: Schocken Books, 1969.

Bersani, Leo. *Marcel Proust: The Fictions of Life and of Art.* 2nd ed. New York: Oxford University Press, 2013.

Carter, William C. *Marcel Proust: A Life.* New Haven: Yale University Press, 2013.

———. *Proust in Love.* New Haven: Yale University Press, 2014.

———. "The Vast Structure of Recollection." In *The Cambridge Companion to Proust*, edited by Richard Bales, 25–41. Cambridge Companions to Literature. New York: Cambridge University Press, 2001.

Compagnon, Antoine. "Lost Allusions in *À la recherche du temps perdu.*" Translated by Jane Kuntz. In *Proust in Perspective: Visions* and *Revisions*, edited by Armine K. Mortimer and Katherine Kolb, 133–146. Urbana, IL: University of Illinois Press, 2002.

———. *Proust entre deux siècles*. Paris: Éditions du Seuil, 2013.

Finch, Alison. "Love, Sexuality and Friendship." In *The Cambridge Companion to Proust*, edited by Richard Bales, 168–82. Cambridge Companions to Literature. New York: Cambridge University Press, 2001.

Henrot, Geneviève. "Mnemosyne and the Rustle of Language: Proustian Memory Reconsidered." Translated by Anthony R. Pugh and Katherine Kolb. In *Proust in Perspective: Visions and Revisions*, edited by Armine K. Mortimer and Katherine Kolb, 105–15. Urbana, IL: University of Illinois Press, 2002.

Jackson, Julian. *De Gaulle*. Cambridge, MA: The Belknap Press of Harvard University Press, 2018.

Jordan, Jack. "The Unconscious." In *The Cambridge Companion to Proust*, edited by Richard Bales, 100–116. Cambridge Companions to Literature. New York: Cambridge University Press, 2001.

Kristeva, Julia. *Proust and the Sense of Time*. Translated by Stephen Bann. New York: Columbia University Press, 1993.

Muhlstein, Anka. *Monsieur Proust's Library*. New York: Other Press, 2012.

Nabokov, Vladimir. *Lectures on Literature*. New York: Harcourt Brace Jovanovich, 1980.

Painter, George D. *Marcel Proust: A Biography*. 2 vols. New York: Random House, 1959.

Raczymow, Henri. *Le cygne de Proust*. L'un et l'autre. Paris: Gallimard, 1989.

Recanati, Jean. *Profils juifs de Marcel Proust*. Paris: Buchet/Chastel, 1979.

Rogers, Brian. "Proust's Narrator." In *The Cambridge Companion to Proust*, edited by Richard Bales, 85–99. Cambridge Companions to Literature. New York: Cambridge University Press, 2001.

Spitzer, Leo. *Études de style, précédé de* Leo Spitzer et la lecture stylistique *par Jean Starobinski.* Trad. de l'anglais et de l'allemand par Alain Coulon, Michel Foucault et Éliane Kaufholz. Paris: Gallimard, 1970.

Tadié, Jean-Yves. Foreword to *Letters to His Neighbor.* Translated by Lydia Davis. New York: New Directions, 2017.

———. *Marcel Proust: A Life.* Translated by Euan Cameron. New York: Viking, 2000.

Taylor, Benjamin. *Proust: The Search.* Jewish Lives. New Haven: Yale University Press, 2015.

Weber, Caroline. Proust's Duchess: How Three Celebrated Women Captured the Imagination of Fin-de-Siècle Paris. New York: Knopf, 2018.

Weber, Eugen. *France, Fin de Siècle.* Studies in Cultural History. Cambridge, MA: The Belknap Press of Harvard University Press, 1988.

SAUL FRIEDLÄNDER is an award-winning Israeli-American historian and currently a professor of history (emeritus) at UCLA. He was born in Prague to a family of German-speaking Jews, grew up in France, and lived in hiding during the German occupation of 1940–1944. His historical works have received great praise and recognition, including the 2008 Pulitzer Prize for General Non-Fiction for his book *The Years of Extermination: Nazi Germany and the Jews, 1939–1945.*

Also by
Saul Friedländer

WHEN
MEMORY
COMES

**A classic of Holocaust literature,
the eloquent, acclaimed
memoir of childhood,
reissued with an introduction
by Claire Messud**

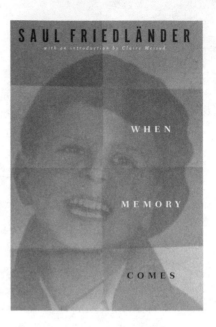

Four months before Hitler came to power, Saul Friedländer was born in Prague to a middle-class Jewish family. In 1939, seven-year-old Saul and his family were forced to flee to France, where they lived through the German Occupation, until his parents' ill-fated attempt to flee to Switzerland. They were able to hide their son in a Roman Catholic seminary before being sent to Auschwitz, where they were killed. After an imposed religious conversion, young Saul began training for the priesthood. The birth of Israel prompted his discovery of his Jewish past and his true identity.

Friedländer brings his story movingly to life, shifting between his Israeli present and his European past with grace and restraint. His keen eye spares nothing, not even himself, as he explores the ways in which the loss of his parents, his conversion to Catholicism, and his deep-seated Jewish roots combined to shape him into the man he is today. Friedländer's retrospective view of his journey of grief and self-discovery provides readers with a rare experience: a memoir of feeling with intellectual backbone, in equal measure tender and insightful.

⊞ OTHER PRESS   *www.otherpress.com*

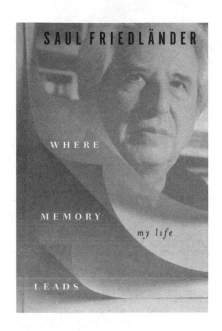

Forty years after his acclaimed, poignant first memoir, Friedländer returns with *Where Memory Leads*, bridging the gap between the ordeals of his childhood and his present-day towering reputation in the field of Holocaust studies. After abandoning his youthful conversion to Catholicism, he rediscovers his Jewish roots as a teenager and builds a new life in Israeli politics.

Friedländer's initial loyalty to Israel turns into a lifelong fascination with Jewish life and history. He struggles to process the ubiquitous effects of European anti-Semitism while searching for a more measured approach to the Zionism that surrounds him. Friedländer goes on to spend his adulthood shuttling between Israel, Europe, and the United States, armed with his talent for language and an expansive intellect. His prestige inevitably throws him up against other intellectual heavyweights, such as Gershom Scholem and Carlo Ginzburg, among others.

Most important, this memoir led Friedländer to reflect on the devastating events that led him to write his Pulitzer Prize–winning masterpiece, *The Years of Extermination: Nazi Germany and the Jews, 1939–1945*.

 **OTHER PRESS**   *www.otherpress.com*